confessions of a wannabe instamom

Heather Lake

First published 2023

www.digimummy.com

Paperback ISBN: 978-0-473-68679-6
Ebook ISBN: 978-0-473-68680-2
Audiobook ISBN: 978-0-473-68681-9

Typeset in EB Garamond and Montserrat

To my Daughters
I love you so much.

And to Dan
Thank you for pushing me across the finish line,
and for making amazing fried rice.

"When despair for the world grows in me
and I wake in the night at the least sound
in fear of what my life and my
children's lives may be,
I go and lie down where the wood drake
rests in his beauty on the water, and the great heron
feeds.

I come into the peace of wild things
who do not tax their lives with forethought
of grief.

I come into the presence of still water.

And I feel above me the day-blind stars
waiting with their light.

For a time
I rest in the grace of the world, and am free."

- Wendell Berry

The Peace of the Wild Things
1968

Contents

Preface

Hi Friends,

Thanks for picking up a copy of this book; I'd love to tell you how it came about.

Five years ago, I found myself in Washington State with two small children, isolated from community and with long, empty days to fill. In that season, God started to speak to me about the way that I used technology to fill those lonely gaps and started giving me a vision of how technology could impact my girls' development as well. The title "Motherhood Unplugged" came to mind one rainy Northwestern night, as well as the sense that for the next five years, I should pay attention to this thought: How does technology impact moms, and how does it impact developing children?

Over the ensuing years, while diapers gave way to preschool and the mountains of Washington gave way to the seacoast of New Zealand, I watched and studied, and I grew in my understanding of how I, as a mostly stay-at-home mom, was hugely influenced by what I saw on my telephone screen. I was influenced by how an influx of influence flew into my children's minds via our television screen and other sources of media as well.

It's magic, these screens we've been given, with the ability to fast forward communication from mail dropped off by pony express to live streaming across continents. But as with all new advancements, there are also some dangerous elements. So I wanted to understand it for myself and my family.

The book you hold in your hands results from this learning, growing, and processing. It's not the book I set out to write, but it's the book that came out when I sat down to write to you. I hope it encourages you that you're not alone in your experiences of adapting to this new world and in your desire to navigate your children through it well. Which we can do, and we will do, and we can walk this part of the road side by side.

Thanks for being here.

Love,

Heather

"This is your realm, the heart of the greater realm that shall be. The Third Age of the world is ended, and the new age is begun, and it is your task to order its beginning and to preserve what may be preserved."

– Gandalf

Return of the King; J.R.R. Tolkien
1955

Introduction

A Brave New World

Recently, I decided to read *The Lord of the Rings.* Living in New Zealand, everything looks like a Lord of the Rings movie anyway. After I read each book, I rewarded myself by watching the film. There was one scene that I've always loved, where Gandalf the Wizard is leading the Fellowship of the Ring through the Mines of Moria. They are accosted by a giant, terrifying, evil dog of fire, and they run across a tiny bridge. Suddenly, Gandalf turns around, thrusts his staff down and shouts, "YOU SHALL NOT PASS!" crushing the bridge with his magic powers. His friends escape, and the fire dog falls into the abyss. Gandalf saved the day. He was running from this great evil and then realized that he was the one who had the power to stop it.

As Moms today, we find ourselves in a similar role. In our homes, we are the ones who get to decide what comes in and what does not. We are the guardians and the gatekeepers of our homes. We decide what food to put in our fridge, what clothes our children wear, and what books and media enter our children's minds. That is our job.

It's amazing. The changes that have taken place since we were young. In my lifetime, technological advances have been rapid, abundant, and very focused on screens and entertainment.

Connection has also been promised to us, but honestly, I don't always feel very connected. Sometimes I feel like I'm losing the ability to have a conversation with my friends, and there is a nagging at the back of my brain that says I'm in a hurry, I need to get back to something, and that my reward for my hard day of work is half an hour of screen time at the end of the day.

Then I wonder, why is screen time my reward? Why isn't my reward a good book or time with friends? Has our modern society made us so efficient that we have hours of free time to fill with junk because there is nothing else to do? I wonder.

I'm a child of the '90s. I remember a time before cell phones, a time before computers. Our first computer that I can remember had a program called "Crayola Art Studio", which was awesome. When the program opened on our large, beige monitor – a song played – "Crayola, Crayola rock" da da da dada. This was so ground-breaking that when the neighbors came over, we took them downstairs to see how the computer "had sound coming out of it."

When I was 16, I got my first cell phone and, in college, I would never be able to be reached by it because I didn't want to carry it around all the time. I liked being "untethered" and free.

Social media entered my world when Facebook was added to my college during my sophomore year in 2004. We were all very excited but had no clue what it was or what it was for. We used it but mostly used our school's "intranet" website with everyone's names and pictures. And we mostly used it to look up the names of boys our friends were interested in. That was our introduction to social media.

Fast forward ten years to when I became a mom in 2014, the world had changed a lot. My phone was an iPhone, and Netflix existed along with internet TV in general. Amazon Prime was the easiest way to shop, and, somehow, people were making rubber iPad cases shaped like animals to give to toddlers.

We are talking about drastic change. It's not all bad change, and it's not all good change. But let's acknowledge that, in our lifetimes; there's been a lot of technological change.

So, what is our role now? As the mothers of a new generation who won't see the world we grew up in because it's gone now, what is our role in leading these children into thriving lives today?

The answer beautifully lies in this quote which is from *Lord of the Rings: Return of the King*. It's at the end of the book when Gandalf is turning over the care of Middle Earth to Aragon, the new King. He says, "The new age is begun, and it is your task to order its beginning and to preserve what may be preserved."

We have entered a new age of the world. The 90s of my childhood were markedly different than the 2000s, and the 2010s were even more significantly different.

As we walk through the 2020s, it falls on us as mothers to order this new digital age. Why? Because we are the gatekeepers of humanity. No adult grows up without passing through the arms of a mother or primary caregiver. Someone must raise all humans. Sometimes it's aunties, grannies, or daddies, but generally, it's Moms. So, this book is for us to order this new age of digital technology in our own lives and for our families.

There has never been an unsolvable issue in human history, and there have been MANY issues in human history. There still are. To every problem and struggle, there is always an answer, and there is always a way forward. Social media, the internet, smartphones, tablets, and smartwatches are all technology.

Technology is not inherently bad. It can be used wisely for the greater good, or it can be used foolishly for more significant destruction. It's an extension of the human self. Just as a skateboard is an extension of my feet, my social media is an extension of my social life. This isn't good or bad. It just IS.

However, certain forms of technology are more potent than others and, therefore, need more strict boundaries around them to be used safely and well. An example of this is the car. A car gets you somewhere faster than you would without it. It's a super fancy horse, a strong bicycle. It's technology. And, used wisely and well, it can hugely propel the human forward. But you wouldn't give the keys to a baby because they wouldn't know how to use them properly.

The internet, social media, and smartphones are powerful tools, and because they are powerful tools, they need strict boundaries around them to be used safely and well.

Mothers today are at an advantage because the wave of the digital age has begun to crest, and we can start to see the impacts it is having on ourselves, older children, and younger children. Much more is known about the effects of social media and screen time than when they were fresh off the assembly line. This is information that we can use to our advantage. But this advantage comes with great responsibility.

Before a child goes to school, ends up at a friend's house for a slumber party, or goes off to high school with a cell phone in her pocket, she is in your home. She is in your care for more hours and days than she is anywhere else. This means you are the primary one who teaches her about technology and the digital age. Not her friends. Not her teachers. You.

You taught her to walk. You taught him to eat. You taught them that they must bathe and brush their teeth. And you are the one who will teach them their digital habits and give them the foundation they will build their lives on.

The ball is in our court.

That is the goal of this book, to hold space for you to consider this time we find ourselves in. The goal is to learn together to think wisely about this area. You can order this new age. You can preserve what can be preserved. You can walk alongside your child as they navigate these unprecedented waters and not send them out to figure it out on their own.

It is possible.

This is something that can be done. You may say that every mother and generation has had to do this. Radios, TVs, automobiles, and every other new technology came with a group of mothers who were parenting at that moment in time, and each group got to decide how to integrate that new technology into their family's existence. And I agree. But that doesn't make it any less important. And this is a specifically tricky terrain to walk. The cliffs are a bit higher, the valleys a bit lower, and the stakes are high worldwide and in my living room.

The internet cannot become our only world. We cannot lose the value of living inside our bodies and connecting with others in person, eye to eye, and knee to knee. This lifetime is the only one they get. This chance to go through school, make friends, bond over silly jokes, write stories, draw, look out the window, dream, and be kids – they only get that once. We refuse to let this life be lost in cyber-bullying, secret unsupervised chats that quickly spiral, or even just the numbness of too many hours of screen face.

We can preserve the best parts of childhood and marry them to the best of the future of what this technological world has to offer. It starts with us and a few foundational beliefs that we can build into our children to help show them the way.

"There's no such thing as a free cat."

– My Dad

Central Illinois; 1995

Chapter One

Welcome to The Attention Economy

When I was about eight, my parents drove us to our friend's farm to pick out two kittens. There was a little pen where piles of roly-poly, fuzzy kittens played and climbed over each other. We picked two—one black and brown beauty we called Muffin, and a grey blue-eyed kitten who would come to be known as Smokey.

They were such beautiful pets, and we loved them. But I remember my Dad saying, "There's no such thing as a free cat." Our friends generously gave us the kittens for free, but Dad was right. Well over a decade of cat food, veterinarian visits, toys, collars, etc., They were not free. While our two pets were worth the investment we made in them over the years, some things that come 'for free' certainly are not.

A few years ago, some people I knew started posting about ways to make money or earn gift cards online. All you had to do was spend your evenings or free time taking quizzes or doing reviews on these websites, and over time you would earn "free" cash or gift cards.

So, one night as a new mom, I sat on my laptop and made myself an account on one of these websites. I sat, and I took the quiz. I quickly realized it would take a lot of time and effort to make any real gains from this scheme. An hour of my quiet evening may make me a $5 gift card, but that was far behind minimum wage—$5 an hour.

Meanwhile, the time I gave up was precious to me; the resting in the evenings to relax, read, or do a leisure activity that would benefit me long-term. There was no such thing as a free cat or gift card; it required something that I wasn't willing to give.

The "Attention Economy" is what experts call the age we live in. It's a time when our attention equals dollars and cents to tech companies worldwide. The way this works is like commercials on TV. Remember when we watched network television and commercials came on between the scenes of *Friends*? Watching TV was free, but we "paid" for the TV show by paying attention to the commercials, and the commercial people paid the TV station for the privilege of showing up on our screens.

This is what is happening in the online world now. We download the Instagram app for free, but how does Instagram get paid? They get paid by advertisers who give them money to show up in our feeds—no such thing as a free social media app.

You get the point.

What is interesting is that children need attention. One educator I know recommends setting aside 15 minutes daily with each child, giving them your full attention. Fifteen minutes a day seems very low until you try it and realize it may not be part of your everyday schedule. But children need attention, one-on-one time, and eye contact to develop, even babies.

There's one problem—children don't have money. In an attention economy where dollars equal eyeballs, kids are broke. They don't have thousands of dollars to spend on advertising to get our eyes looking at them like websites and companies online are. And so, very often, they lose out. They lose out on the attention they need because we are distracted, sucked into the fancy, shiny world of online sparkle.

I bring this up to help us see that we need to be at the steering wheel of where we put our attention. In an attention economy, our attention is super valuable; where we place our eyes and our time is worth billions of dollars to the global tech economy. Still, they are priceless to our developing children, friends, and spouses.
It would be great if we could be in charge of where our attention goes instead of allowing ourselves to float down the stream of online life, especially when our children are around.

Our time is our most valuable resource. Our attention is valuable, and when it is too fragmented—we tend to also emotionally and mentally fragment. The more distracted we arc, the more quickly we lose our tempers, fly off the handle, and get overwhelmed. Everyone is competing for our eyes – especially our kids. So, which is more important? Our children aren't making any money from our attention, but they are making a life off it.

This is a massive struggle for me, especially when I'm tired, which is, of course, during a busy time - right before dinner through bedtime. Here are a few things have helped me along the way.

First, unsubscribe from unnecessary e-mails. It is incredible how quickly a sales or influencer e-mail can skyrocket me into a half-hour scroll or click session. Make a habit of regularly unsubscribing when possible.

Second, put your phone out of sight. Between the hours of 4pm and 7pm is when my family needs me most and when my energy is at its lowest. To take a break, I tend to go on my phone. One way to physically stop this is by putting my phone in a box on a shelf or drawer rather than carrying it around in my pocket. This is an active step I can take so that I don't see my phone and my knee-jerk reaction to "stress scroll" is temporarily thwarted.

Third, practice eye contact. I once saw a video where strangers made eye contact for 2 minutes. It was amazing how much it bonded them and how quickly they could understand each other and become almost instant friends. Practicing looking into our children's and spouses' eyes is a habit that will unveil how they are doing surprisingly quickly. Also, they'll feel so loved that you're giving them your full attention.

Knowing that our children, husbands, and friends need attention and that the "attention economy" is after our eyeballs, I want to encourage us to be selective with our minutes and days.

Being present with those we love is more valuable than many hours of clicks and scrolls, even when it can be challenging to put the phone down and turn off the faucet of distraction.

It is possible, and it is worth it.

"If you feel your value lies in being merely decorative, I fear that someday you might find yourself believing that's all that you really are. Time erodes all such beauty, but what it cannot diminish is the wonderful workings of your mind: Your humor, your kindness, and your moral courage. These are the things I cherish so in you. I so wish I could give my girls a more just world. But I know you'll make it a better place."

- Marmee

Louisa May Alcott; Little Women
1869

Chapter Two

Influencer Culture and Me

In 2003, I was a sophomore in college, and I started a blog on a website called Xanga. My friends and I all did. We sat on our little laptops late at night and typed our words into cyberspace, only to be seen by each other. It was adorable and fun, and safe. Over the years, I continued to blog, writing my thoughts and ideas for friends and family to see.

When I lived in Hawaii, I blogged about it. I moved to Taiwan and blogged about it. Finally, when I became a mom, I blogged about it. I was an early blogger, putting words out into the world since before it was cool. But when I was happily typing in my dorm room, I wasn't "trying to build an audience", "create a platform", or "reach a lot of people." That wasn't remotely a thing. I was writing a journal-type entry to share with my real-life friends.

Fast forward to two years ago, when I started my blog DigiMummy. I've been writing about the digital age for a few years now. I decided to make it my focus, writing for moms about parenting in the digital age and navigating this brave new world with our tiny precious children.

Along with it, I created an Instagram account—DigiMummy, to be a public platform where I could share content I was learning.

Boy, was that a learning curve.

So here are my confessions.

1. There is so much pressure to build a platform and grow an audience when posting publicly.

2. There is so much pressure to look good and take lots of selfies when posting publicly.

3. There is so much pressure to force your daily life to look good for other people when posting publicly.

These may not be true for everyone, but they are true for me. So let's talk about these.

Build a Platform and Grow an Audience

A few years ago, I noticed that many of the ads on my Facebook page were about the "become a coach, become an expert, start a course, start a business" types of things. There were many people out there who wanted (apparently) to help me become a life coach or to start a course or something. No matter that I didn't want to become a life coach or start a business, they would help me UNLOCK MY POTENTIAL and do so for a free online masterclass followed by a pitch for a course that cost $1,299.

What a steal.

More recently, Instagram Reels (Facebook Reels, YouTube Shorts, TikTok) have become a "thing." So now, on my Instagram ads, many people want to teach me how to make reels or do a "30-Day Reels Challenge" to "explode my following" and essentially make me famous.

Isn't that nice of them?

At the end of the day, these are all sales funnels, an attempt to get my e-mail address so *they* can "explode" their following.

There's been a shift from service or social connection to "growth" and "numbers" on social media. And this is because there's a belief that high social media numbers equal success.

So, as a mom at home, typing on her laptop, trying to share what she's learning about parenting in the digital age, I'm also meant to be making reels in my perfectly white kitchen, filming myself—and my children—all the time and posting it to my stories and of course taking photos any time I buy coffee from a coffee shop or walk in nature. It's not enough to create helpful content and give it to the world; I must offer up my entire life for the consumption of strangers so they will feel an emotional connection with me and my message.

And that's not even satire; that's what people are saying. They just say it in a shinier and nicer way.

So that's one pressure, which leads us to the second one.

Look Good and Take Selfies

There is so much pressure to look good and take lots of selfies when posting publicly.

A few days after I started DigiMummy, I'd just gotten ready for a date with my husband. I'd done my makeup and hair, and I had a few minutes before we went to leave. So I went outside and started taking photos of myself. I needed a picture for my Instagram.

As I smiled at the camera, my husband said, "What are you doing?"

"I need a photo for Instagram", I replied.

"Wow," he said and walked away.

To him, it was a cognitive dissonance that to talk about parenting and social media; I had to take lots of photos of myself for social media.

Not that selfies are inherently wrong, but over time, I noticed it was taking a toll on me.

Overall, I've been happy with my face during my years of life. I don't spend lots of time staring in the mirror in angst. I get ready, do my makeup, and move on.

Yet I noticed the more time I spent staring at my face on the screen, the more insecure I started to feel. I began to see things I hadn't before and became hyper-focused on potential flaws and signs of aging that hadn't bothered me.

Then, of course, there are the filters.

In the last few months, especially, there have been lots of videos made "exposing" filters. Girls making videos of themselves with a filter on it and then removing the filter to show their actual (very different but still completely lovely) faces, which has led many of us to realize many people use filters in their online videos and photos.

This is a massive issue for young people today as well. The introduction of face-altering (and body-altering) visual tech (the FaceTune app, to name one) has given a generation of girls and boys the ability to see themselves however they want on their screens. Then, when they come to the mirror, it's not the same; it's devastating for them.

They can essentially create an avatar that looks real by adjusting their features and changing their appearance. Or they can put a beauty filter over their face for their content online. Or they can make their faces look older or younger. (Not to mention that unsafe adults can also do this to make themselves look like a 14-year-old teen when they are a 45-year-old adult.)

For some, this has led to them pursuing plastic surgery, altering their authentic selves to look more like the filters and edited photos.[1]

How sad is this?

It's very sad, and I understand how they feel. I know the pressure to make your images and videos look good online, to get attention and "build an audience", and then feel like what you see in the mirror isn't good enough.

This is part of why I'm so against social media for young people because an image-based social connection app has some natural slippery slopes, such as image modification and the subsequent insecurity in real life.

I remember the first time I saw an ad for one of these image-altering apps. It began with a photo of a girl, then with a slider button. Her eyes grew larger, then turned blue. Her skin darkened. Her hair grew longer. Her eyebrows shaped. Her chin line tightened, neck lengthened. I remember thinking (in my 30s) I never want to use that app. I want to like how my natural face looks. I don't want to feel like my real face looks bad in comparison. Also, I want people who see me in real life to think I look like my photos, and I don't want them to meet me or see me in real life and think, "Oh wow, she looks so different."

I'm not saying selfies or filters are bad, terrible things. However, these are some things to consider for ourselves and be aware of before we let our children use them. That's all. I want my two girls to like their faces; to like the way God made them; to think that they are so beautiful and lovely, just as they are. And I'd prefer not to expose them to something that will teach them something else. And that's fair. Even the cute little "animal ear" filters add makeup and eyeliner and smooth out the skin. So if our little ones grow up seeing themselves on mommy's phone like this, we are subtly teaching them to use these filters and to like how they look in them rather than loving how they look in the mirror.

Marmee said it best in *Little Women*: "If you feel your value lies in being merely decorative, I fear that someday you might find yourself believing that's all that you really are."

Ah, now we've arrived at the biggest bone I have to pick with the Insta-Mom movement—the pressure to make your life look amazing for other people.

Force Your Daily Life to Look Good

There is so much pressure to force your daily life to look good for other people when posting publicly.

Imagine if your mom was a family vlogger in the 80s and 90s. And when you were at your 4th birthday party, she was filming everything, making videos of herself talking about the party and your friends and all your gifts, and filming the food and making it look perfect for the world. What would that have felt like? It would have made me feel like my life wasn't mine, that it was for everyone else. It would have made me feel like the people on the phone were more important to my mom than I was.

But this can happen when we let other people's opinions of our lives become more important than those who live in our homes, who rely on us for everything.

Let's carry the birthday party story out a little more. A friend of mine used to be a children's party planner, and she posted about how she decides how to orient her parties. She said that if she was planning a "Princess Party," her goal was not just to stick photos of Disney Princesses on everything. Her goal was to stage and create the party so that the children at the party felt like they were princesses themselves. So instead of focusing on the party's image and how it looked, she asked, "What would make them feel like princesses?" It's a focus on value and feeling rather than simply image.

So when we're thinking of the online content we'd like to share, it's also essential to consider the children in our homes and how our actions impact them. They are not props in our lives to make us look good.

It's better to get two pictures of a party that a child enjoys, or on a Disney Vacation or a weekend hike, than to spend the entirety of "family time" smiling into a screen with our backs to our kids or with our phones shoved in their faces so they can't even see our eyes. We are modelling appropriate behavior around phones and family time to them. So if we spend all of our time recording, posting, and scrolling during family time, we're absolutely teaching them to do the same.

So what do we do?

The essence of this topic is Images vs. Values. How things look is less important than how it feels to be somewhere. How you look on a particular day is less important than what you see, what you notice, what you smell, and what you hear.

So, as we instruct our children step by step through this world, let's focus on the values we hold dear, the way we want to see the world, rather than just how we look walking around.

Take some time to consider these questions:

- Have I allowed how things look to become too important to me?

- Am I drawing my value from how I, my family, my home and my life look to others?

- What would I prefer to draw my value from instead?

"If you look at the world,
you'll be distressed.
If you look within, you'll be depressed.
If you look at God, you'll be at rest."

\- Corrie Ten Boom

Chapter Three

Trying to be Everywhere at Once

A few years ago, my friend Sarah told me about a book called *In His Image* by Jenn Wilkin. This book discusses different attributes of God and how we do not have to be all those things. It listed a quality of God, like Omnipresence (being everywhere at once) and talked about how God is like that and we are not.

As I read this book, I was struck by the differences between us and God and how we feel pressure daily to be things we cannot be.

Let's begin with omnipresence, feeling like we must be everywhere simultaneously. Why do we think this? For starters, social media or traditional media like TV, movies, or the news can quickly show us what other people are doing, like magic. Then we think, "Oh, man, I should be doing that, too." For example, some of my friends from college went on a beach holiday together recently. A few years ago, I may have thought, "Oh, I'm jealous. I wish I could be there." But now, knowing I can't be everywhere at once, I thought, "I'm so happy for them."

What about "All-Knowing" or "Omniscient"? God knows it all. He knows how many hairs are on our heads, the day we will die, and what we ate for breakfast. He knows everything. But we don't, and sometimes we wish we did. So, we research, Google and

Wikipedia until we're blue in the face because we don't like not knowing everything. We read the news obsessively, ensuring we don't miss a single breaking story. We don't want to miss out.

The thing is, we can't know everything. We have a limited capacity. We can only do a few things at a time. We can learn some things, but we won't ever know everything. And we can very easily overwhelm and even depress ourselves or breed anxiety when we "doom scroll" and try to know it all. And why do we try to understand it all? Because we want to feel safe. If we know it all, then we're safe, right? But in fact, exposing ourselves constantly to external input can (and does) harm us. It hurts our peace and mental health; it can remove our joy of the moment and replace it with overwhelm, fear, anxiety and sometimes depression.

I never really read the news before the pandemic. If something was necessary, I figured my husband or my sister—who watches CSPAN for fun—would tell me about it. And they did, and I was fine. But then, suddenly, things could change on a dime, and one headline labelled "LOCKDOWN" could drastically alter our lives in a moment. The government in New Zealand did daily updates at 1pm, telling us whatever new thing we needed to know. So, we watched the updates, and I read all the news.

Something interesting happened to me. The more I knew, the less I felt I knew, and the less safe I felt. I wasn't safer or less safe depending on what news I read, but I felt less secure because, suddenly, I was deluged by so much bad news.

There was also good happening in the world, but that wasn't the kind of thing showing up on the news websites. In an attempt to know everything, I became depleted and afraid rather than trusting God to take care of us.

It doesn't have to be this way. A way to read the news healthily is to keep it in proper perspective and balance it with other input sources. Corrie Ten Boom famously said, "If you look at the world, you'll be distressed. If you look within, you'll be depressed. If you look at God, you'll be at rest."

I've found this to be true for me.

The fear of being accused of "having my head in the sand" has sometimes caused me to over-scroll, over-research, over listen to everybody everywhere else. I want to be aware of the trends, the critical political movements, and even the new ideas of my family and friends that they post online. The reality is, however, I am a human with a limit on my time, energy, brain capacity and emotional capacity. I will miss some things. And I get to choose what those are.

And I don't want to miss the essential things in my life, like the story my daughter wants to tell me after school, or the late-night confidences that come up right at bedtime, or any of that because I'm so plugged into what's happening in other places, and other homes, to other people. Feeling guilty because we can't keep up with it all may be the norm, but it's not right. We can only keep up with some things; we were never meant to participate in every event happening globally every day. We were meant to trust, worship, follow, and listen to the One who can.

I am a woman under influence, and I am a woman with influence. My influence is in my home, with my children, with my family, in my community and real life, as well as the circle of writing and work God has given me with Digimummy. I am under the care of the government I live under; I choose to obey the laws set for me, pay my bills, and to respect and listen to those given the task of stewarding the place where I live. I will be the most influential when I operate within my sphere of responsibility and influence. I will be the least influential when I refuse to do the work before me that's been given to me and spend my time stepping out of that sphere, criticizing others or being distracted by what they are doing.

Obviously, we speak up for injustice. Obviously, we deny tyranny. Obviously we fight for what is right, but we do this in the context of our sphere of influence and responsibility, not as keyboard warriors fighting in the comments on someone else's social media post.

Finally, the main issue of "omnipresence" that bothers me is returning to social media and what has come to me to be known as "the worship of the algorithm." This will sound absurd in 10 years. Still, at the moment, a popular strategy taught to social media platform builders is to figure out what "the algorithm" wants and give it that. *Dictionary.com* defines an algorithm as "a process or set of rules to be followed in calculations or other problem-solving operations, especially by a computer."

This means that each social media website, built-in computer code, has built within it a set of rules or a process to determine which content to show each person using it. When I log into YouTube, Facebook, or Instagram, the computer code can decide which photo, video, or image I will most likely click on, like, follow, or watch. It's a computer program that keeps me on the website for as many minutes as possible to sell my eyeballs to advertisers and make money intermittently.

Creators are now attempting to essentially "court" the algorithm so that it will show its content to as many people as possible. And thus, many "experts " have made it their job to teach other people how to exploit or use this technology to get their message in front of as many people as possible.

This is not good or bad. It just is. It's a technology that people can use for good or evil, like a car. A car is a tool, an invented technology, it can be used to drive you safely to school pick-up, or it can be used to crash into a building. The driver is the deciding factor in how well a car is driven. Computers and digital technology are the same; we can use them for good or bad, to connect or to isolate, to create or to overwhelm. We are the deciding factor here.

The algorithm, designed to serve humanity, now has much of humanity serving it.

I'm not a computer, but I'm supposed to act like one to get my message out to "the world". This means posting on a schedule, regularly "showing up", and on some social media at least "showing up" in stories every day so that people who click on my page "know that I'm there."

This creates a tremendous amount of pressure that humans can't sustain long term. The stress of "you need to post, or the world will forget about you because the algorithm won't show them your posts unless you live on this app every 10 minutes of your life" is not healthy for us.

Last night my husband and I watched a documentary about an MIT professor who is creating ways to make buildings sustainably.

She said, "Nature doesn't produce. It grows."[2] We are more like nature; we grow in seasons and out; we have dormant seasons where we don't produce anything and sudden seasons where we make a lot.

We are not computers. Computers are an imitation of us. We are created beings, more like an apple tree than the YouTube algorithm. And when we try to be all things to all people in all places and at all times, our limits will remind us that we cannot.

I also don't love that this kind of tech leads to more extreme and polarizing content because people want to be seen, so they get louder, and their content intensifies. More extreme means more comments, which means the algorithm notices—"Oh, people are engaging on this post; let's show it to more people." The algorithm wants constant content to serve customers, and tends to show them the more extreme, loud things.

Let's talk about how this leads to deep thinking and well-thought-out discussions between people with a few opposing views. Oh, wait... does it? No, probably not. But it does tend to lead to reactive, shallow, angry posts and, eventually, reactive, shallow, angry people.

That's sad. Because we got on social media in the early years of Y2K to connect with friends, and now we're just sitting on our couches watching conspiracy theory videos on Facebook. Well, not necessarily, but the truth is that all of this "pressure to be present all the time" and "pressure to please the algorithm" has built a giant wall around people made up of strangers who may not even know what they are talking about.

This leads us to echo chambers. An echo chamber is a cozy little room created by Betty (the algorithm) for each person, full of articles, videos, and posts that closely align with their beliefs OR, for a bit of fun, posts that directly oppose their views and make people who differ in opinion to them look like morons. Pardon my French.

People could live in an echo chamber at any time in history. Cults, for example, have existed for a very long time. Still, social media and the rise of polarizing press, in general, have exacerbated this human condition.

A few months ago, I got into an echo chamber on YouTube. I clicked on one video, and the next day a similar but slightly more extreme video was offered to me. I immediately realized that I was on the cusp of an echo chamber, and, honestly, those kinds of videos have plagued my YouTube feed to this day. I was self-aware enough to realize that I was getting myself into something, but I'm not always, and I'm not immune to the impact of them.

Echo chambers don't usually impact me in an empowering way; instead, they steal my energy and brain space away for relatively fringe issues. I need my emotional energy intact and full to raise two little girls in this world, to keep my home running smoothly, and to build into my marriage. I don't need it stolen by a 90-second clip on a hot topic issue.

The reality is everyone online is at risk of getting into an echo chamber at some point or another, which is why it's essential to keep connected with people in real life and make sure to spend time on long-form content as well as short-form.

The TikTok algorithm is one of the strongest in the world. Even a slight hover over a video will lead quite quickly towards the same kind of content but more extreme, according to a study[3] done by the Wall Street Journal. It is well worth a read if someone you know and love is using that app. It's a purpose-built echo chamber machine, full of massively harmful content alongside the funny prank videos and cats. User beware.

So, the idea of ever-presence online has led to some dark places, and it's not how we were built to live. Humans have more in common with nature than with the devices we use. Just like trees bear fruit in season and go dormant in the cold winter months, we were never made to create, create, and produce new content daily, hourly for our whole lives. This is why many YouTubers quit from burnout after a few years on a daily or weekly posting schedule.

You can still have a consistent posting schedule if that's what you choose to do and can do. However, you don't have to listen to the pressure of "Betty the algorithm" to be the boss of you. You can be free, bear fruit in season, and still impact your world. Consider if there are ways that you're trying to be "like God," trying to be everything and everywhere for everyone. How about, instead, you lay it down and ask Him what He wants of you in this season and let Him guide you with wisdom?

So what do we do?

A strategy that's been helpful for me is to wait to read the news or even check social media until after noon as much as possible. I learned this strategy from Susan B. Arico. I find myself to be so malleable, so soft, so spongey in the morning time. I wake to find my soul hungry, desiring food, rich, authentic, good food.

And when I feed her flashing lights and the worst things that have happened in the world first, it can make her sick and afraid. If, instead, I provide her excellent music, peace, Scripture, and an encouraging written word first thing in the morning, she is better equipped to handle the torrent of the world later on.

Often I need to check my e-mail before 12pm, which can lead to scrolling through everything else. So another idea is to stay off social media and the news (or whatever drains you) until after reading your Bible or another encouraging book. I love the Bible in One Year App, and usually tap it to start it playing the moment I drop the girls off to school in the morning. You can listen to it as you drive and fill your soul before diving into what everyone else is talking about online.

"Food is for eating.
Places are for being in."

- Ron Swanson

Parks and Recreation
2013

Chapter Four

SERVICE VS. CELEBRITY

In August 2019, YouTube Influencer Sierra Schulzie walked into BeautyCon in Southern California feeling like a million bucks. That's also the exact number of how many YouTube subscribers she had—one million. A few hours later, she walked out discouraged, frustrated, and completely toppled. She posted a video called "We were treated like Absolute Garbage at Beautycon", referring to the disregard and flat-out rudeness she and her producer/ best friend were treated with during the conference.

When Sierra waited in line to have her photo taken in the behind-the-scenes "VIP" area that she had been invited by BeautyCon to be in, the event staff denied her entry. When she walked the red carpet, she was ignored.

Sierra is a YouTube star and has a massive following. She does videos about fashion, body confidence, and other fun topics. She is a delight to watch. But this Beautycon thing put a microscope over an interesting issue for me.

In the footage that Sierra shared from Beautycon, it was clear that everyone there focused on one thing: how they looked.

This was why Sierra and her friend were so uncomfortable. The entire atmosphere of the event seemed to be "Me. Me. Look how amazing I am", and the resulting environment caused Sierra (and I am guessing lots of other people) to feel like they didn't belong. No one feels comfortable in an environment where everyone is focused on themselves and their image or, in this case, "beauty".

Celebrity culture for the average Joe is a new phenomenon in human history. We have always had heroes and people to look up to—Great warriors, leaders, orators, and kings. Humans have always looked up to other humans, usually for their accomplishments and skills that made the world better for the weaker, the poor, and those on the margins of society. We've also always had plays, actors, and even wandering poets, but they weren't necessarily lauded the way celebrity entertainers are now.

With the invention of the film camera came films and then movie stars. The advent of television created television stars. The rise of the internet has made internet stars (and a myriad of hopefuls willing their days away in front of a screen, hoping to raise their subscriber numbers beyond their close friends). Kids, teens, and adults seeking to pitch their tent on the mountaintop called "celebrity".

A recent study said 1/3 of children today say their future career goal is to be a YouTuber[4]. That's a lot of children, and it's worth exploring. First, how do they even know what YouTube stars are? To grow up wanting to be a firefighter, you have to know what a firefighter is. When I was a preschool teacher, we took our 3-to-5-year-olds to the fire station in town to see the big red fire truck up close. The tall, kind firefighters bent down on one knee to talk to the children and explain what they do and why they do it. More than one child left the fire station that day with a new dream: to be a firefighter.

When I was 18 and off to college, I studied teaching because when I was in 2nd grade, my teacher told me that she had decided that SHE would become a teacher when SHE was in 2nd grade. So, I decided to do that, too.

We're easily influenced when we are young, and these early choices can impact how we see ourselves and the lives we choose to craft for ourselves. So, when children watch YouTubers and build emotional relationships with them, it affects the life they see themselves living. Now, I understand the desire for fame at a young age. If I had been a child when YouTube was introduced, I could see myself starting a YouTube channel and making videos. But I'm glad I didn't.

Why am I glad?

Because I was protected and safe within a world, my parents could create for me, in a world where I had genuine relationships with the real people in my life. I learned life skills, like conversation and how to set the table, and I got to drift into the world of books like Anne of Green Gables and Little Women. I got to be a child.

I think "service vs celebrity" is an interesting crossroads that our kids stand at when choosing their life trajectory, and one framework to put over this is this: What is the goal? Is it seeking a CELEBRITY image of what life could look like (fast cars, big houses, fancy clothes)? Or is the goal seeking a life that provides SERVICE to others based on a certain set of values?

Imagine a little girl from your neighborhood. She sits at home and watches YouTube videos, and decides she wants to be a YouTube beauty star. She tells her mom, and her mom says,

"Ok, fine. Go for it." So she spends hours in her room making videos, trying on outfits, creating content, learning to edit videos, and watching make-up tutorials. Her life becomes about her image, brand, opinion, and personality. Her life becomes increasingly about HER. She vlogs about her life, her tastes, her, her, her.

And even once she reaches the top, what awaits her? What will she find once she reaches a million subscribers? 10 million? If she reaches them at all. At what point will she realize that now that she has a platform, she has nothing worthwhile to say? At what point does this no longer become a viable option for life once youth and beauty fade?

Imagine this same little girl from the same home. She sits at home and reads books about Nelson Mandela, Corrie Ten Boom, and Mother Theresa. She decides she wants to make a difference in her neighborhood. Her mother encourages her, tells her she can do it, and introduces her to community leaders she can learn from. She studies. She spends her evenings writing papers, and she does well in school. She goes on to university, where she gets a good degree. She volunteers in her local homeless shelter, studies, reads, learns, and gets a job in her community serving the people who need it most. She has dignity in her work, and she has something to offer.

Experience and age add further influence to her, not less and less. She becomes a community leader, a role model; head held high. She became what she beheld.

Now, can a child watch YouTube videos and read quality books in one lifetime and live a whole, impactful life? Yes, absolutely. But the key is - where is their focus? What is the child's heart being set on?

These two women in our illustration were created because of a mother's decision. A mother allowed the first girl to watch YouTube videos to become so enamored with the lifestyle of an "influencer" that she wanted to become one herself. The mother in the second scenario fed her daughter different long-term fuel. She equipped her to become a woman who could make a difference in her world and, in the end, give dignity to herself as well.

What about us? Will we train our children towards celebrity or service?

I'm not imply that celebrity cannot align with service, but one has to lead. The service and purpose element must lead, or emptiness of life will inevitably follow.

It seems harmless, YouTube, the influencer thing. But I don't think it is. Watching influencers can become a substitute for real friends, and becoming a content creator without any drive of service or mission behind it can, for children and young people, become an emptiness that spirals in on itself.

When I was growing up, my mom told me that when you walk into a room, try to be a "There you are!" instead of a "Here I am!" person—walking into a space focused on other people rather than on others seeing ME.

Sierra's experience of walking into a room full of "Here I am, look at me" people was empty and unsatisfying. She said that she went to other conferences that were much better, that were fun and worth her time. BeautyCon was not that way, and that's not surprising. The event was not about inner beauty. It was about appearances, and it was not satisfying and fulfilling to participate in, regardless of what advertising or images portrayed the event as being. It was a room full of people who spent their life building up their image—how they looked—and, as Sierra found, a bunch of them in one place created a very shallow, empty place to be.

I have two precious little girls, and I want them to have fulfilling lives. I want them to have something to offer and contribute to the world. I want their inner beauty to be as developed as their outer beauty.

So, my questions are these: How are we preparing our children for a life of service and creativity? Are we preparing them to contribute to the world, to have something to offer and give, to live a life of dignity, and seeing their and others' self-worth? Or are we preparing them for a life of image worship and personality cults?

One way to answer these questions is to notice what kind of media they consume.

We become what we behold. This is another wise thing my mother used to say to me. We become like what we see. We become like the things we watch, the books we read, and the people we spend time with.

When my girls were younger, it did not take long to pinpoint a particular attitude or sassy habit to a show they had been watching. Children are sponges. They soak up every little thing they see and hear. These days, if there is a whiff of sassy talk or mean-friend talk in a show, I turn it off immediately because if they watch it, I'll be parenting that attitude for the next six weeks. I don't let them watch behavior that I don't want to have to parent out of them. It is not worth it.

Izzy's Koala World is one of the best children's TV shows I've ever seen. Izzy is a young girl living on an island in Australia with her parents. Her mom is a vet, and they run a clinic where they tend to rescue sick or injured koalas. Izzy is living the dream, getting to cuddle the little koalas, feed them, and even play with them in her room while being supervised by her very responsible, gentle, kind, knowledgeable mother. Izzy rides her bike around her community, searching for the perfect eucalyptus leaves for koalas who are struggling to eat, and she is very involved in helping to rescue these small fuzzy creatures.

Honestly, I wish every children's show was like this—slow paced, real people, real stories, and a focus on doing something beneficial in the world.

What a vast difference between the influencer life of unboxing videos and overdramatized monetized life events.

When choosing our children's media, let's think about this—will this focus my child on "image" and therefore encourage them to pursue looking and acting a certain way? Or will it influence them to use their days and life in service to the world?

Finally, I'd love to share a story about Lisa Kudrow, who famously (and brilliantly) played Phoebe on *Friends*.

In an interview[5], she shared about realizing that she could be an actor without being a celebrity. She could do the work of being an actor, using her gifts to serve the world in the entertainment sphere, without going to all the parties and doing everything the "celebrity life" is about. She could do her job and be home for dinner with her family. And I'm so glad she did because when she uses her gift, it's incredible, she is a fantastic actor. But even for her, the focus was never an image-focused celebrity goal; it was to do the work of being an actress. This is a sentiment that other famous people have shared: they almost wish they could do the work of acting without the hassle of fame and the celebrity because it is the work that they enjoy; the celebrity is just something that comes with it.

Lets not let our children chase an empty (albeit sparkly) chalice. Sober-mindedly guiding them towards work, service, and careers that they enjoy and can use to bring value to the world will be much more satisfying over time.

It could be teaching marine biology, and they may use their YouTube channel to communicate or prepare or serve information online. Maybe they'll produce or act in movies or share their music with the world. But helping our children put their focus on using their efforts to serve and create in the world will be far better for them long-term than letting them chase engagement numbers and likes online.

Practically speaking, this means asking questions like, "Why do you want to do that? Who would you like to benefit from the work you do? What problem would you like to help solve in the world?" And then offering them experiences and ways to explore these things as well.

"ALL OF HUMANITY'S PROBLEMS STEM FROM MAN'S INABILITY TO SIT QUIETLY IN A ROOM ALONE."

– BLAISE PASCAL
1654

Chapter Five

What's an iPhone?

In July 2011, I attended the last big event I would ever participate in without a smartphone in my purse. My little sister's wedding.

The other bridesmaids and I wore light blue, flowy dresses, while my sister was the loveliest red-haired bride in her long white gown and veil. I may have had a camera, but the only photographs I have of the day are the professional ones done by the photographer. I have a few scattered memories of the events, specifically the song during the ceremony and my little cousins dancing like absolute wonders during the reception. I was present, healthy, and engaged for the entire day, and we all had a great time.

In the years prior, my husband and I had been living in Taiwan, working as missionaries doing non-profit work and Bible teaching. Around this time, some of our co-workers returned to the United States. They went to the cell phone store to get new phones.
"Would you like a smartphone?" they were asked.
They looked at each other and then at the salesperson, "What's a smartphone?" The clerk looked at them as if they were from another planet.

We had missed smartphones up to that point (my sister's wedding), having served overseas as missionaries for the past three years, so we were well behind the curve. Along with our friends, we'd all been happily walking around Taipei with our "candy bar" phones (phones that looked like candy bars) and were none the wiser.

After the wedding, we planned to drive from Illinois across the country to Montana, and the maps app on an iPhone was much more exact than the old GPS we were using. So we got iPhones.

Facebook was old news by that point, but we'd always accessed it on our laptops and found that sufficient for keeping us connected and logged in for plenty of hours a week.

Now, smartphones entered our lives. I was 27, newly married, and would become a mother in the next two years. I remember sitting in my car with my first iPhone in the car door pocket and thinking, I must maintain my ability to sit quietly, stare, and think. One of the great joys of my life has always been sitting and staring, just thinking (or not thinking!).

When I was a pre-teen, I remember telling someone, "One of my favorite things to do is sit in my room and stare at a wall." They probably thought I was strange, but sitting, thinking, reflecting, and daydreaming had always been a massive part of my inner life. I had a rich inner world that I loved decorating with new ideas, pondering and sorting out my trains of thought, and deciding which things went where. It truly has been one of the great joys of my life.

I remember that day, sitting in front of the building in Montana where my husband worked, in the front seat, waiting for him, thinking to myself, "I must keep this. I must keep this ability to sit, wait, be peacefully quiet, and just be."

I must have already felt the tug of the connected life, the buzzing siren song of the phone in the car, and known that, in fact, it could wipe that part of me away.

Of course, it did, or at least sure tried to.

While I was busy fighting my battle to maintain my inner life, thousands and thousands of young people were doing the same thing, but they lacked something that I had—life experience and a developed adult brain.

When the first generation of young people was handed smartphones, some were too young to remember a world before, a world before the internet, a world where staring into space and daydreaming was normal. Well, mostly normal. And because they had no way of balancing their newfound technology privilege with established habits of solitude and deep thought, they struggled.

At the time of this writing, it's been a little over a decade since the iPhone and its compatriots became ubiquitous in human life. 2012 is said to be the time smartphones became mainstream, and the impacts of this started to be widespread.

In *Digital Minimalism*[6], Cal Newport lays out eloquently the mental health struggles that increased quite drastically at this same time, namely anxiety.

Before 2012, mental health in teens and young people had been steady. There was a slow decline in mental health and a slow increase in mental illness but nothing like what happened after 2012. There was such a sharp, drastic upturn in anxiety, depression, and suicide in teens that it sparked many studies and articles. Massive evidence supports the theory that smartphones and social media intermingled in the hands of teens drastically impacted the lives of teens in a highly negative way.

Research is slow, and the only way to have research is to have tests, test subjects, and controlled environments. However, it's not too late. As an adult, I've struggled so profoundly with smartphone and social media habits. I don't think it's just social media. It's the twitchy, unavoidable urge to check my phone, like a phantom limb. It's like Bilbo with the ring in the *Fellowship of the Ring*, "It's been growing on my mind," and it's extremely obvious to me.

Being present in life is one of my great values, especially with my children, but when I'm tired, weak, in pain, or unwell, my phone offers a distraction from this. It provides a nice little, "Hey, try this," and effectively "erases" my pain for that moment.

The science is clear about why this happens. The overstimulation on the screen causes dopamine to rush into my brain and dopamine wins. It flashes through my nerve endings and makes me feel better. After a time, these dopamine flashes are followed by the reverse effect, which makes me sad. To recalibrate my brain's chemistry, my body starts to flood my brain with hormones to reestablish the proper balance, and I can feel myself sinking into sadness.

I never know which I'll get, though. I might feel better, so, almost like a drug addict, I return to the source, hoping for a win.

All of this is terrible for my parenting skills, as a burst of tears or emotion from my child is too much for my now quite hyper-stimulated, overwhelmed brain and emotions to handle.

And I'm an adult.

I'm nearly 40 years old, with an active interest in the science of technology, and I have fallen into this trap too many times, to the point where I have deleted my Facebook over and over and have had to put stringent guidelines on myself with other phone and social media use.

What makes us think, then, that the developing mind of a pre-teen or teenager is equipped to handle this brain re-arranging technology with no arising issues?

It's not.

Even if it's not depression and anxiety (although the statistics show that it probably will be), there will inevitably be a shallowing of thought as our children paddle through the insipid moment-by-moment trends of TikTok or stare yearningly into another YouTuber's video or click through more and more inappropriate videos until they find themselves addicted to pornography.

The unguarded internet is not a safe place for children. Social media is a massive door into the internet, and smartphones, with their flashy apps, make social media extremely hard to resist.

But, something IS possible. There ARE ways to communicate and connect to the world without typical smartphones and social media, and they CAN be found everywhere. The developing brains of our children need protection from technology like this so they can develop properly. Not just individually but also socially and collectively as a group.

Simon Sinek[7] stated that developmentally, middle schoolers deal with a lot of emotional changes and difficulties, and the reason for this is so that they will bond with their friends. They have this challenging part of life, and this is the part of life where they start to develop strong bonds with their peers. They are supposed to take their pain somewhere, and these bonds begin their foundation of social life as they grow up. They also should be reaching out to parents, trusted adults, teachers, and coaches now.

Yet now, more and more, young people are retreating into their phones. Instead of bonding with the people in their lives, they connect with content creators and influencers in a one-way relationship that will not lead to positive social lives later in life.

So, what do we do?

We say no. We don't give our children smartphones. We don't let them use social media until they are developmentally ready (late teens at the earliest), and we explain why (because they are addictive, and we want to give your brain time to develop before introducing these things into your life). Then, we fill their lives with real connections, honest friendships, fun activities, hobbies, good habits, and so much real life that they don't miss it.

What about peer pressure?

The peer pressure will be intense, but the more we talk about this with our communities, the parents we know, the parents in our children's classes, and at church. In the places where our children live their lives, the easier it will be because if most parents say no, then most children will begin to think that this is normal.

What about us?

I've recently been trying to get more quiet time and silence into my life, so I've tried something I'm calling "Silence Stacking". Here's how I do it. Before I turn on the TV in the evenings or pick up my phone, or before I turn my podcast on during a walk, or before I turn on the radio in the car, I pause. I give myself a few minutes of silence or quiet to think. Before I let the world into my rest, I take a break, take a beat, and let the thoughts flow around and out. Sometimes, I enjoy it so much that I keep my phone or the TV off the entire time. But I'm trying to build a habit of sitting quietly peacefully again and ignoring the siren song of the outside world when I'm resting, bit by bit and reclaiming my brain space from the thousands of bits of information clamoring for a place to pitch their tents.

I'm inviting you to join me too.

"It would be a relief in a way to not be bothered with it anymore. It has been so growing on my mind lately. Sometimes I have felt like it was an eye looking at me. And I am always wanting to put it on and disappear, don't you know, and wondering if it is safe, pulling it out to make sure. I tried locking it up, but I felt I couldn't rest without it in my pocket. I don't know why. And I don't seem to be able to make up my mind."

– Bilbo Baggins

The Fellowship of the Ring; J.R.R. Tolkien
1954

Chapter Six

Why We're Addicted To Our Phones

The year was 2003, and the place was my sophomore dorm, Burritt Hall, Greenville College, Greenville, IL. There was a new kid in town, and its name was Facebook. We'd heard about it; all the "cool, big" universities had it, while we'd settled for the less awesome MySpace. But, now, it was here. Greenville College was allowed passage into the wonderful world of Facebook.

We joined immediately, "friended" each other and started to upload photos from our camera SD cards onto our computers and into Facebook to share. The lighting was dim, the images were blurry, and we... did not care. It was what would become "the good old days" of social media. If it were an album, it would undoubtedly be called "The Early Years."

Over time, Facebook grew up, and so did we. As our social circles expanded, both online and in real life, our Facebook friend count grew. There were rumblings and murmurings on the outskirts of our conversations like "I'm addicted to Facebook" or even the occasional overly dramatic "Facebook is evil". But we never took any of this seriously, not really. It was a fun little place to talk to friends and share photos.

This continued happily for a decade.

Imagine my surprise, finding myself as a young mother, nursing and rocking my baby to sleep in 2014, when I realized that I might be addicted to this thing. I certainly used it as a regular habit. Screen addiction wasn't a thing. Nobody was talking about the mental and emotional potential for harm with social media, but I slowly started to feel drawn further into the social media world.

I couldn't go a day, sometimes an hour, without checking my Facebook, scrolling for hours in the evenings through other people's vacation photos, baby photos, Etsy shop links, and other random things people shared. I found myself slowly detaching from the world around me and, in that "early mother fog," finding it hard to connect with the people around me. Instead, I found solace in the constant scroll and buzz of the online world.

Previously, I'd been an active part of real-life social networks, bouncing to work and back again, but now, at home with a newborn baby, it was harder to go out, make plans, and find out when my friends were free to hang out. It was effortless to stay home and connect online, clicking here, clicking there, chasing the elusive high of the red notification button.

As I grew, and my children grew, this early connection of motherhood and social media as a source of solace tracked with me. When we moved to a new state with a one and 3-year-old, I had only one real friend in my new world and long, windy, rainy days to fill.

Each time I moved after that, social media was the thread that connected me back to my roots, old friends, new friends, and the community I had long left behind in the real world. It was great. I was so thankful for those connections, but I couldn't shake the feeling that something was wrong, that I was spending TOO much time "hanging around" Facebook and not enough time creating a new life.

So, I started to read. I began to read about the internet and addiction and what the internet does to our brains. I made it my quest to figure out *why* we are so addicted to new technology and *why* I couldn't shake this Facebook (and later Instagram) habit that I could feel was not helping me after all.

Social Media is Designed to Hook Us

In his 2016 TED talk "*Why you should quit social media*"[8], Professor Cal Newport discusses the addictive technology of social media and how he, as a young student, refrained from using it in a fit of professional jealousy, which turned out to be the best decision he could have made.

Cal talks about how the people who make social media studied gambling machines to help them understand how to keep people online as long as possible. Slot machines receive a coin and, at random, offer rewards. The rewards need to satisfy the user more for them to walk away. Instead, the random patterning of rewards keeps them hooked, returning repeatedly. This is similar to how a bag of chips keeps us reaching for more; we aren't nourished or satisfied, so we keep reaching for more.

This happened to me and my girls the other day. A claw machine filled with soft toys is at the foot of the escalator by our closest supermarket. We have walked past this machine for four years, and my firm "No" has kept my coins in my pocket. I'll never know why I folded this particular day, but I said ok, "let's try," and we tried.

Four dollars later, we were no closer to cuddling a new soft toy, but one of my girls was hooked. She'd had *nearly* won the stuffed llama and was determined to try again. Again, I don't know why I said yes, but a few days later, with a coin in her little purple pocket, we were back. Again, we failed. Again, I folded, and we spent over $10 to take home the elusive stuffed animal behind the glass.

To make matters worse, we happened to be walking by one day when another child did successfully get a llama from the claw machine, which proved to us that it is possible. The "there might be a reward" was enough for us to keep trying. This is true of gambling, and this is truly the way social media companies have designed their applications.

The little "red heart" on Instagram, the little "red tick" on Facebook, even a new e-mail, all of these programs have a way of alerting us and our impressionable brains that there is something new for us—a shiny new toy, a yummy new brain treat—if we click on the button. Then our brains are "rewarded" with something funny, sweet, and simply *something*. The reward is useless, our brains simply know there is a reward.

Social media applications are designed with the intent to keep us coming back again and again. Why? Because our eyeballs on the screen result in their ability to sell advertising slots to people selling things. It's become a game of eyeballs = dolla dolla bills. So, they want to make their programs as compelling as humanly possible. So, they do, and as a result, we're hooked.

Sad Scrolling

In the book *Irresistible*, Adam Alter discusses why we get addicted to social media, and he calls it a behavioral addiction[9]. Essentially, the crux of the issue is this: when we are unhappy, and we go to something to make us feel better, we can get addicted to the momentary hit of happiness. So we keep returning time and again even if it doesn't make us feel better after a while. This is great news because does it mean we can use social media when we feel fine and won't get addicted to it? Maybe?

Remember, social media is designed to hook us so that it will be more challenging, but maybe it's possible. It's a relatively new technology, so we're still figuring that out here. The point is, when we go to this stuff when we are feeling low, we are far more likely to get addicted to it, which means we're unable to stop using it.

Let's be honest, how often do we go to social media and our phones when we feel sad, tired, or upset? How often can it be our stress response? A lot, I think.

Connection Seeking

Our brains are wired to seek connection and check on our social lives, even when our brains are trying to rest. When our brains are resting, they go into "default mode"[10], and a few things happen in "default mode". We mentally check on the stability of our social networks, do problem-solving, and do creative thinking.[11] So, if we aren't doing anything focused, if we aren't on a specific task, one of the things our brains do with this "free time" is check the stability of our social lives, check our friendships, and see how we are doing with the people in our lives.

This is a good reflex. However, when it's transferred into a social media context, our brains will almost constantly encourage us to check social media because it's such an expedient way to check on our social networks (or so it seems).

Social media addiction is real, complicated to combat, and can be solved, but it takes intention. So, think twice before setting up an account for your kids, and consider if there are some ways you might need to mitigate your use in favor of healthier, richer real-life or just more analogue connections. It is possible to live a whole, rich life in the digital age, and the more we understand how it operates, the easier it will be for us to make wise choices for ourselves and our families.

Recently my 20-year high school reunion took place in central IL. I found out about it via a Facebook page started by our class president. Social media helped to organize the event. Being a huge fan of high school and loving the people in my class, I wished I could be there, but the reality of living in the middle of the Pacific Ocean meant I couldn't get there. So I saw photos and pressed "like" and hoped to be able to get there next time.

After the event, I messaged a friend who was able to be there to get all the details of how everyone was. She encouraged me to download Marco Polo and we started video messaging. She gave me the down-low on how it all went, updated me on our classmates' lives and fam ilies and children, and then we talked about other things, our upcoming move, our families, and homeschooling ideas. It was much more fulfilling and enjoyable to have a conversation than just "like" photos posted to a large online audience. This continues my belief that not all social media is created equally.

I logged out of my Instagram today to focus on writing, and the login page said, "Log in or Sign up to see videos and photos from your friends." But that's not what I see necessarily on Instagram. I see some of that, but I also see a large amount of photos, videos, and ads from people I don't know, which fractures my attention repeatedly and habitually.

We must weigh each social media and technology that crosses our paths. It's not cut and dry. Without social media, my classmates might not have been able to invite me to our class reunion. On the other hand, somebody could have tracked me down if they'd tried hard enough.

As we approach social media, we need to know the deck is stacked against us. The platforms are literally hijacking our brainstems to keep us on their apps, so if we do choose to engage in their world, we need to do it carefully, and we have some clear boundaries.

So what do we do?

First, take a break. Long stretches of abstaining from social media have been a lifeline for me. When my children are home in the summer - no posting on social media because posting gets me scrolling, wondering why my posts don't get enough likes, wondering whose posts are getting likes, and what the trends are. I get sucked in. Refraining from posting on vacation or weekends helps a lot.

Many experts suggest a regular Sabbath or rest from technology. Some even suggest a rhythm to follow throughout the year. One hour a day. One day a week. One week a month. One month a year.

Taking a rest from social media gives us a chance to step back and regain access to our own minds and thoughts. Sometimes the best way to see clearly is to rest from the flashing lights and endless scroll of bright videos on our phones.

Second, unfollow and Unsubscribe from people or accounts that drain me.

If there are accounts or people whose posts are draining me in a particular season, I stop following them. If social media is supposed to be something encouraging, fun, and connecting, I delete accounts that aren't that for me.

Third, try turning my screen to black and white

If my screen is black and white, it's MUCH less fun to look at, and I'm far less likely to scroll. This is the best tip in this whole book. Figure out how to turn your phone onto greyscale, which will become much less irresistible.

Fourth, quit social media altogether

I've never met someone who has deleted their social media and regretted it. I've met many people who spend tons of time on social media and regret it. Suppose you stop using social media to connect with the people in your life. In that case, you may be surprised to find how much more motivated you are to seek connection in real life when that loneliness isn't lowkey satiated by a constant shallow scroll.

Chapter Six Grace Note:

In the Berenstein Bears book "*Too Much Television*", Mama Bear decides the cubs, Brother and Sister Bear, have been watching too much TV, so she decides the entire family will have a "no TV week." At the end of the book, Brother Bear asks, "Mama, what is it you don't like about TV? What do you have against it?" Mama replies, "Goodness, I don't have anything against TV. I like it. What I'm against is the TV habit - sitting in front of it day after day like old stumps waiting for dry rot to set in."

The same is true with smartphones and social media. They can be used well and wisely, and the better we understand how they work, the easier it will be for us to create healthy habits.

"All true trophies of the ages
are from mother-love impearled,

For the hand that rocks the cradle
is the hand that rules the world."

- William Ross Wallace
1865

Chapter Seven

Generations and Gatekeepers

I sat up in the middle of the night, feeding my new-born daughter Sadie. An old rocking chair my Mom had found for me cradled us both, a little bookshelf my husband made sat beside me, and my phone was in my hand. I was texting my friend who'd just had her second child. I knew she'd be up, too. She was.

"What was the name of that special swing you had?" I texted. "My Little Snugabunny Cradle and Swing," she replied.

Whenever I had questions or felt alone, I messaged her, and she wrote back in those early days.

I don't remember what else I did during those sleepy, wakeful nights, but I remember that my phone was my constant companion while I nursed my sweet baby. It was always there, always available, a lifeline to help when needed. In that season, I was thankful for that.

I knew my daughter needed eye contact when awake. I knew her little eyesight focus only reached a few inches from her face in the crook of my arm to my face. So, when she was awake, I put my phone to the side and looked into her little eyes, watching her sweet nose, cheeks, and lashes. But, when she nursed and slept, it was just me, my sleeping girl, and the whole world online.

What should have been a benefit sometimes wasn't. Sometimes, it wasn't great that my close companion was the "all-powerful" internet during those days because sometimes what it fed my young, tired, naïve Mommy eyes wasn't what I needed to hear or see.

Images of perfect moms in the cutest neutral outfits, the ideal diaper bag ("see what's inside my diaper bag"!), and smiling faces were everywhere. Before Sadie was born, I researched, and Amazon shopped and made the ideal Target baby registry. I was convinced that everything else would be okay if I had the right things. A consumer mindset was instilled into me during those early days.

I don't know how many "must-have baby" blog posts I read, but I believed them. I thought that if my motherhood *looked* a certain way, I would be a good parent. And I was desperate to be a good parent. A subtle mindset whispered in my ear that motherhood was an image that looked a certain way rather than being a set of skills to develop or even a relationship to cultivate.

Fortunately, I also had good friends who were already Moms around me who could say, "You do not need a wipes warmer" or "You actually might want to get this kind of baby carrier," but I also had the other loud voices in my ear – the voices of the online world.

Beyond the "stuff," there was another element to becoming a new mom in the digital age, the element of fear. There were many articles about safety and all the risks of everything when I was pregnant and a young mom. Thou shalt put no toys in the baby's cot. Thou shalt put no blankets in the baby's bed. Thou shalt put your baby on its back only. There were so many "right" ways to do things, which carried over into more than sleep. It is carried into foods as well. Certain foods were the "best" to start with, "or else your baby's life will be ruined forever," is how it felt.

There were so many rights and wrongs and so much stress about doing it the right way all the time.

This is still true today with older children, although the messages have changed. Do you know what parenting messages (best practice for how to be a parent) your screens scream at you torrentially? What are they? Can you bring them to mind?

New moms are at a very stressful point in their lives. Often separated from family support, covered in baby goo, and with little time to care for ourselves, we turn to the online world for connection.

I was recently babysitting my friend's precious six-month-old, and I got to have a peek into that world again.

I sat, snuggling his little 6-month-old self as he drifted into a dream. My friend asked me to babysit her son for the morning, an opportunity I'd willingly grabbed. We had a morning of mat time, played with chewy toys, and giggled. When he got tired, I picked him up and rocked him back and forth in front of the window. Heavy rain poured down outside as we watched the traffic drive by, and I looked out to sea. A few moments later, I looked down, and he was asleep like a baby koala.

I walked over to my favorite blue armchair and sat, rocking and soaking up the baby cuddles. My husband came upstairs after a meeting and smiled at the sight of us. It'd been a while since we had a baby in the house, five years, to be precise. A deep peace filtered through the air, and I closed my eyes and breathed, taking in the rest and the break time, relaxing into the moment of peace.

My mind drifted back to when I had small ones like this, memory straining to remember what it felt like to hold my small girls, being a new Mom, trying to figure it all out, the long, somewhat lonely days when our world was small and revolved around our living room.

Trying to see how it would feel to be a new mom again, I picked up my phone and tapped on Instagram. I typed "#newmom" into the search bar and started to scroll. What was it that new moms were being fed today? I wondered. And how would it have affected me as a new mom?

Immediately my screen filled with pastel squares, gorgeous pregnancy photos, and staged product placement images with smiling blonde moms dressed in white on blankets at the beach. My heart rate quickened. My eyes flickered across the photos, searching for something to help and encourage me in my imagined "new mom" state. You know the feeling.

After a few minutes of scrolling, my eyes slightly overwhelmed, my husband came in again with my two girls, who had been home sick from school, resting downstairs. Instead of finding a sanctum of peace and calm as he had before, he found an irritable, slightly frustrated mess. I snapped at his request and lost my temper at being interrupted.

What had happened? What had quickly taken me from peace and rest to irritability and stress?

Simply put—I'd used my "down time" and "rest time" to overstimulate my brain, and now I'd flung my attention to all corners of the world. In a quick, short turn of events, I'd exchanged the contentment and peace I'd been soaking in for the images of other people's ideas, their best moments, their sales pitches, and aspirational quotes. Research shows us what happens when we are bored—our brains at rest become their most creative. But how can we find our creativity when we are so busy filling our minds with other people's ideas?

Looking back on my early mom days, I feel sorry for that sweet, earnest, tired girl who just loved her baby and wanted to rock her to sleep but couldn't because the internet and some book said so. Don't want to spoil the baby.

My oldest is eight years old now, off on a day at the zoo with her Daddy so Mommy can write, and, sitting here now, I wish I could have told myself then that there is more than one right way to do things.

I was in the "mom cave" of tiredness and survival. In some ways having constant access to the world wide web didn't help. The "experts" and the "mommy bloggers" (which technically I am one) each had their agendas and things they were trying to put out into the world, and I gave them too much credit. If it was in black and white, they were right, and that's not always the case.

We have access to so much information at any given moment. But this has also not always been the case. So, to carve out some perspective together on this, let's dig into the past. Let's go back in time to a big old house in a small town in Iowa. This is my great-grandma's house, where my grandpa grew up.

As we go through these seasons in time, I want you to imagine what it would have been like to be a young mother in that time of the world. Who were the gatekeepers of parenting information? What would the rubric for success have looked like for you? Who decided if you were "doing it right" or not?

When my Great Grandma Irene was raising her children in a small town in Iowa almost 100 years ago, she had lots of advice, but it was localized, personal, and relational. She had neighbors, friends, and people she knew from church and the community who would have come around her and helped her. She wasn't alone either, and she probably got competing advice, but it would have been bantered out over a quilting bee (quite literally) or around the kitchen counters while making a big family meal. It was based on both reality and relationship.

When my Grandma Roma was raising her children in Central, IL, in the '50s and '60s, there were also people around her. The advice had probably changed by then, and she may have had some women's magazines to read, a few parenting books, and maybe newspaper articles about parenting, but they were fewer and far between. There may have been print resources available to her.

Yet her primary source of information about parenting still would have come from people she knew, her Mom, her friends, her neighbors, and her maternal instinct.

When my Mom was raising my sisters and me as babies and small children in the 1980's in a house in the north of Normal, IL, she had many resources. There were books on parenting, some conferences for Moms, friends, family, and community, radio shows, and some recorded conference audio tapes. She had access to print and audio resources. The external input would have been more common, but still, her primary source of information would have been people she knew, genuine, living relationships, and personalized help and advice.

By the time I had my first baby, it was 2014 in rural Montana, and what felt like limitless resources were available to me. The internet existed, which it hadn't when I was born and raised, meaning that 24-7, I could access print, audio, and video content telling me what I needed to be a "good healthy mom."

Anyone could make content, whether they were an expert or another parent or just a human with a laptop and an internet connection. It overwhelms me to think of the massive jump in the information from when my Mom had me to when I had Sadie, one generation.

I think this is the abiding legacy of the internet age—overwhelm. So much information, so many people clamoring for attention and eyeballs, and those of us trying to raise families wanting so much to do the right thing and give our attention to them.

There were undoubtedly amazing people around me; friends, other moms, and my family, who helped and advised and gave me relationally-based, personalized help, and assistance when I had small children. Many of them still do.

The new factor for my generation of moms, though, is that those voices now have to compete with many other, ever-present, ever-louder voices and images of the online world.

Here is a recap of the Gatekeepers of Parenting Resources and Support over the Last 100 Years:

The 1920s and Great Grandma—Relational: Personalized help from people they knew where they lived, a bit of print possibly available; Gatekeepers of Information: Family, Friends, Neighbors.

The 1950s and Grandma—Relational: Personalized help from people they knew locally where they lived, plus a bit more print and maybe books (newspapers, women's magazines); Gatekeepers of Information: Family, Friends, Neighbors, books, newspapers, and women's magazines.

The 1980s and Mom—Relational: Personalized help from people they knew locally where they lived, lots of print resources (books, magazines, newspapers), some audio resources (tapes, radio shows; Gatekeepers of Information: Family, friends, neighbors, books, newspapers, tapes, parenting conferences with experts, and radio.

The 2010s and Me—Impersonal via Facebook, Mommy Blogs, Parenting Websites, Pinterest, Amazon online shopping, online news, the general internet of things, plus books, magazines. *Plus* relational, personalized help from people I knew where I lived, *and* online help from people who I know across the entire face of the planet *and* all the additional resources they might find or have or post about on a possibly daily basis; Gatekeepers of Information: Family, friends, neighbors, books, the internet, social media, and bloggers.

The 2020s and New Moms Today—Precious young mothers today have the added pressures of TikTok, Instagram Reels,

YouTube shorts, and family vlogs and videos, podcasts, Snapchat, as well as Facebook, Mommy Blogs, Parenting Websites, Pinterest, The general Internet of things, plus books, magazines, and also relational, personalized help from people they know locally where they live, AND online help from people who they know across the entire face of the planet and all the additional resources they might find or have or post about on a possibly daily basis; Gatekeepers of Information: Influencers, YouTubers, people who post online, friends, neighbors, family.

Try saying that last list ten times fast. It's a lot. So many sources of information are available to young mothers today. Times have changed, and honestly, it's made us anxious Moms. Maybe not you, but it's made me a more anxious Mom than I would have been otherwise.

Knowing everything that could go wrong made me worry that those things would go wrong. I think learning about every kidnapping (and being able to research for hours everything about every past kidnapping ever), knowing about potential health issues, and knowing about just all the things that could go wrong is not the healthiest for me.

On the other hand, there are massive benefits to having all this information at our fingertips. I have three friends who figured out their child's significant health condition thanks to their internet sleuthing, which meant their child received the help they needed. This is a life-changing benefit. We couldn't have done that before.

Globalization certainly has given toward us as well. That's why we use the internet because there are massive benefits to be had. However, there are side effects to misusing the internet, including anxiety, depression, isolation, fear, comparison, and feelings of failure. This is why we are talking about this. It is just good to lay it all out there and say, "Hey – you know what? We are dealing with a massively altered world, different from what the women before us experienced, and we need to be wise about how we engage in it."

That means trying to be self-aware of how much undue influence I give to people I don't know and who don't know me.

On beautiful summer evenings when the sun is still high, my children are in their beds (not sleeping but having been put to bed), and my husband is on the couch, I slip out the back door to walk at my local beach. It's a short walk across the road, down a secret pathway, along another street, around the corner, and then, boom, I'm at the beach. I slip off my flip-flops and leave them under a bush. I let my bare feet relax into the smooth, cool sand.
I walk along the beach, past the Pohutukawa trees, past huge beach mansions and little "baches" until I reach the sailing club. Then I spin on my heel, take a deep breath, and slowly walk back up the beach.

I look out over the sparkling waves, take in the sun-tinted clouds, and wonder at the beauty of "What even is my life right now?" and listen to her. My favorite podcaster. I love her encouragement and listen to her regularly. It's truly amazing how often she says just what I need to hear, and I genuinely believe that God uses her ministry of speaking to speak into my life and what I need to hear. I will continue this routine and absorb truth and wisdom from her.

But one day, after struggling and listening to her almost every day, I realized she doesn't know ME. She doesn't know and speak to MY specific life, children, and person. I also realized it had been a while since I called my Mom. I'd been needing to, wanting to. Still, I'd been filling my need for an actual person with this podcast which maybe was fine, but, over time, what I needed was a relationship, someone who knew me, who saw me, who knew my kids, and who could speak into my life with love and truth that was relational and personal.

So, I called my Mom. She didn't answer. I live on the other side of the planet to her, so the time difference can make it difficult sometimes. I kept trying until I got her on the phone. And it was what I needed; she could pour love into my heart as no one else could. Maybe for you, it's a friend, a mentor, a sister, but, the point is, we need relationships with real live people, alongside the encouragement we get from people we don't know.

It's wonderful to get encouragement from people online, in books, and in various places. But we also need input, love, and thoughts from people who know US and our specific situations, experiences, lives, and children because we need real-life first-person connections and support from people who know our story.

So what do we do?

Consider this question: Who am I listening to, and why?

A massive reason for isolation for new and experienced mothers can be listening to voices online at the expense of in-person relationships. We all need people who know us and our circumstances and who can speak into our lives.

Remember that we don't have to agree with someone on every little thing to be in a relationship with them. Your grandmother may give advice that isn't 100% the same as the influencer online, but that doesn't mean we should dismiss what she says. Being willing to hold the tension between current trends and long-held wisdom and try to receive from both is wise. If someone gives you advice you don't like and even maybe won't do, you can still smile and say "thank you" without feeling like you must cut them out of your life altogether.

We won't agree with everyone in our real lives all the time. However, long-term, life-long relationships are still a valuable part of a whole and healthy life, offering perspective outside our "bubble" that might be helpful later along the line.

New moms (and experienced moms) need to develop in-person relationships with more experienced parents and their peers. The online world is so full of information, and we need moms who have done their race to give us perspective on what is truly important and what is a trendy wind.

Finding a regular playgroup and committing to going as often as possible was helpful for me, as was finding a mom's group that I could go to twice a month. If you can add regular, repeatable, relational rhythms to your life, that's easier than setting up a new playdate with a new person every week. Try to find rhythms you can plug into and commit to going for a few weeks or months, even if it's initially uncomfortable.

It's not about finding the perfect community; it's about creating connections over time that can become our natural life support when needed.

"Painting is complete as a distraction.
I know of nothing which, without exhausting the body more entirely absorbs the mind."

- Winston Churchill

Painting as a Pastime
1948

Chapter Eight

Stress Knitting and How Hobbies Can Help Us

We lived in Washington State for a year while my husband completed his Masters. The girls were six months and 18 months old when we moved to a new town where we didn't know a soul. A few friends lived the next town over, but we were alone in the world apart from then.

During this time, I found myself with a new hobby called "stress scrolling." I would be physically tired from being up early with small children, existentially tired from long days alone and socially tired from lack of stimulation. So I would spend extra time on social media as a stress response and relief.

One day, realizing that my social media time wasn't helping me, I laid my current knitting project on the counter where I could see it. Then, whenever I felt stressed or bored, I could pick up my yarn and needles and knit a few rows. My breath would slow, and my attention would return to the current moment while simultaneously giving me a break from my present moment.

It was magic.

A similar thing happened to me during the pandemic. Long days with young girls at home sometimes left me feeling socially isolated and restless. During this time, I entered my "baking era." I'd never loved baking but wanted something to do with my hands. I wanted the dough to pound and knead and put my energy into it, so I did. I learned to make a new kind of bread that required kneading. I wrote out my favorite cookie recipe and froze bananas for banana bread.

Over time, when I felt the "afternoon angst" at 2pm and the long day still stretched before me, I would put my phone down and head to the kitchen, get out my flour and baking soda and ingredients and make some dough. I'd invite the girls into the kitchen, cover their hands in flour and let them go at the dough as long as they wanted. This "stress relief" activity was productive, connective, and relaxing.

Throughout history, women have done work with their hands. They've embroidered, planted, worked the earth, made jams, churned butter and cooked food for their families. I sometimes wonder if we miss out on not needing to do this. We can buy ready-made bread, clothes, curtains, and everything we need. We don't have butter churning to get our stress out with. This is tongue in cheek, but it's worth considering that our elevated modern-day stress issues may stem from a lack of physical hobbies in our homes.

The loss of leisure activity is a big one. We need leisure activities, not just leisure, "sitting on the couch doing nothing." (Although I also like to do that. But it's about balance.)

My friend Shannon and I organized a women's event at church a few weekends ago. It was called the "Art of Belonging." We did art journaling, and heard a beautiful message about how as women, we long to be and to belong. Shannon shared with us about the benefits of art journaling, and it was so interesting.

Art journaling is good for our focus, emotional health and creative thinking. Some of those benefits include helping us think more clearly because we can put the thoughts inside our heads on paper. Also, creating art activates the reward pathway of our brain[12], meaning that we feel good and perceive it as a pleasurable experience. This feeling is what social media and many digital experiences attempt to mimic.

Finally, art journaling helps us focus deeply. Creating art can put us into "flow", which activates networks in the brain such as a relaxed reflective state, concentrated attention to task and a sense of pleasure. This means that simply creating art has actual benefits that can cause us to focus more on the rest of our lives.

One study found that visual self-expression, which means making something with your hands, literally increases blood flow to the reward center of your brain.[13] In the study, participants brain activity was monitored while they participated in three different artistic activities; doodling, free drawing, and coloring. The study showed increased brain activity in the reward centers during each exercise. In this same study, a survey was done before and after the activities, polling participants on their self-perceptions of their "abilities to have new ideas, good ideas, a good imagination, and novel ideas and about their ability to solve problems" Overall, they judged themselves higher in these areas after doing their art, especially in believing they could have good ideas and their ability to solve problems.

Not only did doodling, coloring and free drawing signal to their brain that they were having a good time by activating their brain reward center they also felt more able to solve problems and have good ideas afterwards.

Before learning about these benefits, taking the time for myself to watercolor or draw seemed like a waste of time. I longed to spend more time being creative but felt guilty doing it while the piles of laundry I needed to fold stared me in the face. Shannon's words made me feel free to spend more time painting and creating.

It's interesting how one change can impact other changes. I'd love to say I never stress-scrolled again once I took up painting; however, that's not the case. But hobbies and leisure activities can plug into our lives and make them fuller, creating more fulfilling habits than watching short videos online in our free time.

This is true for our children as well. One of the greatest gifts we can give them is leisure activities, hobbies, interests, and skills. Developing these skills takes place over a childhood, over a lifetime, not overnight, but it can be a goal we aim for. We can introduce them to different activities, sports, the arts, and music and see what interests them. Doing so gives them a head start in life, so when they grow up and find themselves overwhelmed, they might find themselves dipping a paintbrush into paint or tinkering on a piano because that's what they've been taught to do. Emotional regulation isn't just taking deep breaths; sometimes, it's also giving our pain a creative outlet, giving our aches a voice, and training ourselves to go for a walk or shower when we find ourselves overwhelmed.

I remember watching the episode[14] of The Crown, where Elisabeth is crowned queen. In this episode, this episode, her uncle, Prince Edward, Duke of Windsor, cannot attend the coronation because his wife, was not invited. On the day of the big event, he is at home with his wife in France, and after watching the new Queen receive her crown, he is overcome with emotion and goes outside, where he plays his bagpipes into the wind, tears in his eyes. I remember thinking how good it was that he had an outlet for his emotion. Whether this was factually true or not didn't matter. The idea still rang true that it is a good idea to have and to instill into our children's methods of creation and activity that can help us to express our emotions into the world. Artists and musicians have been doing this for time immemorial, and it is such a gift to turn our joy or pain, fear or jubilation, into art.

Hobbies have been one of the great joys of my life, but they do take some effort to learn. It takes a bit of effort to set up a home where it's easy to grab a board game, grab paper and paints, and set up a piano or drum set. But this effort will be well rewarded in our lives and the lives of our families.

Do you have a hobby or leisure activity that you enjoy? How easily can you access it when you need a moment to calm down or stress relief?

Consider making a basket of things you need for your hobby and placing it in the main living area of your home. Place a good book within reach of where you sit in the evenings. Set your paints on the table, pull your running shoes out of the closet and put them by the door. Hunt down your scrapbooking papers or rock-climbing gear and put it where you can see it.

You're more likely to use it if you can see it.

If you don't have a hobby or leisure activity, consider what you might enjoy doing. How can you take baby steps towards learning something new or re-kindling something you once enjoyed?

"There is no fear in love, but Perfect love drives out fear."

- John

1 John 4:18
95 Ad

Chapter Nine

No Fear in Love

When my oldest daughter was seven, her school required her to have her own Chrome Book, a little laptop she took to school daily. This terrified me. She was seven, a tiny child, and now I was expected to send her off for 6 hours a day to do who knows what on the actual internet without me around. This seemed like a wild, ridiculous thing to do. The school, of course, would be supervising them.

My daughter had a wonderful, responsible teacher who watched them closely. They were never allowed to "do whatever they wanted", and while I discussed my concerns with the school whenever they arose, it was fine, and the school did a great job monitoring the students. But what was interesting was the amount of fear that this experience stirred up in me.

I had a conversation with one of the teachers at the school about it before the year began, and she said to me, "Heather, what are you afraid of?" Wise teacher.

I was afraid she would see inappropriate content.
I was worried that she would lose some of her innocence.
I was fearful that she would lose her literacy and ability to do handwriting.
I was afraid.

I was able to protect her to a massive extent when she did not have internet access, but with internet access, who knows what would happen?

But even if something did happen, I would need to respond with love, not fear.

During this season, God gave me this verse, "*There is no fear in love, but perfect love drives out fear.*" – 1 John 4:18

Over the past few years, I've talked with many parents about the online world, smartphones, and digital tech, and often the conversation ends up swirling around the teenage years and the fear that looms there.

There is fear of what it will look like when their child goes to a slumber party, and everyone has smartphones and is doing who knows what. There is fear of what other children will show their children on a screen on a dark bus ride home from a basketball game. There is fear that their child will be cyber-bullied, meet an online predator, or become addicted to social media or porn or video games.

We have a lot of fear, and it's not all unfounded. It's based on the reality that, for many parents, these are real things. How do we approach this next stage of life, where our children will be exposed to something we cannot control?

I think we drop anchor here—there is no fear in love, but perfect love casts out fear. We confess our fear to God, bring him our requests, pray, and ask God to guide us and give us wisdom as we navigate the digital age with our kids.

Let's talk about what fear does.

Fear isolates. When it came to my daughter having to have a computer at school, fear isolated me. Fear made me think of all the bad things that could happen, but it took away any agency I had to deal with those potential outcomes. Once I gave my fear to God, I was able to approach it from a calm, rational standpoint.

What was I worried would happen, and what could I do to mitigate those concerns? What questions did I need to ask the school? What resources could I draw on to help me figure that out?

I messaged *Protect Young Eyes* on Instagram and asked for advice. I talked to other parents about what their experiences had been. I met with the school's tech advisor and asked him many questions. I could approach it, not fully without fear but with less. I was able to enter the conversation.

During the year, when something came up, I did respond with a bit of fear, talking to her teacher in a way that was a fear response rather than a love response which her teacher was very gracious about. However, I later wished I had done it differently.

Fear separates us from people and causes us to isolate, and hinders us from moving forward well.

Another way that fear has impacted my motherhood journey is the fear of going out unless everything was "just so." A sliver of fear slipped into my heart somewhere between the piles of laundry, the dishes in the sink, the scrolling social media, and the desire for a true relationship.

Somewhere along the line, I feared going out into the world with my precious little ones without looking right, the children behaving well, and being properly prepared for any circumstances. This meant that I sometimes felt trapped in my house because I couldn't do all those things all at once.

I remember living in Washington State when the girls were small. Sadie was 2. Elsie was a baby. We had just moved to a new town, to a new state. I didn't know anyone nearby. My family lived in Illinois, across the country, and my husband was away studying for his masters degree most of the time.

After moving away from our Montana community and neighbourhood, I became an isolated suburban Mom overnight. And there, in that townhouse with two small children, I felt like I couldn't "go out" into the world unless I had my ducks in a row, which I never did. I joined a "Moms Facebook Group" for the area, but it was neither helpful nor edifying, so I promptly left.

But why did I feel I had to have it "all together" to engage in the world? Partly because of what I saw online, where it seemed everyone had it all together. Therefore, to engage in the world, I had to have it all together too.

A few years later, after we'd moved to New Zealand, I joined a music and movement group of moms with young children. It was a "come as you were" kind of place I'd needed in Washington. It's what every mom with young children needs – a place to come as you are, baby spit up on your shoulder, toddler food on your jeans, go as you are. In reality, none of us have our ducks in a row, but sometimes we think everyone else does. Social media tends only to exacerbate this.

I remember seeing a friend's social media post where she seemed completely happy and at peace, all was good in the world, and she was having a great trip. That night, I got a message from her, full of concerns, worries, fears, and frustrations with things that were going on. Without the message, I would have assumed everything was wonderful, and I wouldn't have known to pray for her. I might even have been tempted to be jealous of her. But in the context of the relationship and her message, I could see a fuller picture of how she was truly doing, which meant I could pray for her, and she didn't feel so alone.

What we see on social media can create rifts between us and our friends because a) we assume they are completely fine and don't need our support due to their "perfect pictures" and b) it can cause us to be afraid to bring our true selves because their lives seem so great and ours seem so bad by comparison, so we withhold.

And that doesn't lead to true friendship at all.

Fear can separate us from other people, and sometimes fear is fed to us through our screens; fear of the future, fear of other people, fear of what might happen to our kids, fear of what might happen to us, our families, or our marriages.

So what do we do?

When fear starts to whisper or has us cornered, isolated, doom scrolling all alone in the kitchen at night, what do we say to it?

Firstly, find out the truth. It's important to find out the truth of the situation. "You will know the truth, and the truth will set you free."[15] I was worried about what my daughter would see, what would happen with her device at school. So I pursued the truth, asked questions, confronted my fears, and tried to get at the root of them. I found out the truth of what exactly was happening at school and engaged in a conversation. Once we know the truth, we can deal with the situation far more easily.

Second, focus on love, not fear. When we find ourselves responding in fear about what the future may be like for our children or being afraid that technology will "take over" or absorb our children, ask God to show you the truth of the situation, and then ask him to replace your fear with His love in that situation. "There is no fear in love, but perfect love drives out fear."

I find it helps me to write it down, journal it out. Write down what you are afraid of, and specifically pray about that, and ask God to give you wisdom and guide you.

Finally, we must continue to pursue a relationship with the people in our lives, regardless of how they look online, irrespective of what they post, what echo chamber they've found themselves in, or if their political stances differ from ours. No fear in love; perfect love drives out fear. Confess your fear and learn again to walk in love in your real life. Cast aside fears stoked by half-truths on your screen.

"It's nicer to think dear, pretty thoughts and keep them in one's heart, like treasures.

- Anne Shirley

Anne of Green Gables, L.M. Montgomery
1908

Chapter Ten

The Grid and The Treasure Box

The fluorescent lights of the big box store lit up the bright white floor and tall packed shelves, and I was on a mission. Today, I was going to buy a sketchbook. I wanted a book full of blank pages for practice sketching. I noticed a grid book as I walked through the aisle of blank journals and sketchbooks. Instead of blank pages, it had hundreds of tiny squares, a grid traced across each page.

This was a breakthrough. In my attempt to teach myself to draw and paint, having straight lines in place could help train my muscle memory and eye to create straight lines when needed. Horizons – instantly easier to draw. Houses – Yep. There are a lot of times in drawing when having a grid could be helpful. Also, the grid notebook was $1.69. Score.

Driving home from the store, I started to ponder what would happen if someone created a grid notebook like mine, but the lines were off. What if the lines were slightly off, tilted, crooked, or not straight? What if the little squares were squiggly or triangular? Well, it wouldn't help me make straight lines, and if I trusted those lines, my drawing wouldn't be right either. This happens when we expose our children to poorly created media. They receive a skewed vision of the world, an inaccurate representation of how it works, which will influence how they see it.

Angela Santomero is the creator of *Daniel Tiger's Neighborhood*, *Wishenpoof*, and *Blue's Clues*, among other shows, and she talks about the importance of appropriate television in her book *Pre-school Clues*. While her focus is on 3-to-5-year-old children, parents of children of all ages can benefit from her depth of insight.

In her chapter on "Modeling", Santomero introduces the concept of "peer modelling." This is the idea that what children see modelled by their peers, they will absorb and want to attempt as well[16]. She then explains that the characters in the shows that children watch count as "peers". Children see the characters in their TV shows as their friends. (Let's be honest, I do this too! Hey Lorelei and Rory!)

In the 1960's Albert Bandura and collegues from Stanford University conducted a series of experiments called the "Bobo doll" experiments[17]. The Bobo doll was a weighted doll that would stand back up when knocked down.

Researchers placed children into two groups, one group watched someone model violence towards the Bobo doll, and the other group watched someone model non-violent behavior towards the doll. This was also done in 3 different ways, a live actor, a short film of a live actor, and a "cartoon-like film" of a live actor wearing a cat costume.

After watching this film, the children were made to wait in a room filled with toys they could not play with to elevate their frustration levels. They were then put in a room with the Bobo doll and some other toys, some "aggressive" type toys, like dart guns, and "non-aggressive toys" like tea sets and dolls. The results were "astounding." Those who saw the aggressive behavior modelled exhibited aggressive behavior. The aggressive behavior occurred whether the child had seen a live actor, a film of a live actor, or a cartoon-like image. They not only modelled the behavior but also made it more extreme, using the other toys in the room more aggressively and adding their aggressive acts.

Santomero also added a positive modelling example.[18] She notes, "When Sesame Workshop put a sticker of their iconic character Elmo on an apple, researchers at Cornell University found that children ages 8-11 were 65% more likely to add an apple to their lunch than when the apples had no stickers."

I've seen this in play with my girls as well. Walking around a big box store one day a few years ago, we all noticed that Elsa was on everything; lunchboxes, water bottles, pyjamas, everything. It almost felt beaten into me that Elsa was the queen, and we all needed to bow down.

My girls were too young to watch Frozen, but by the time they did, they'd seen so many images of Elsa and Anna that they would have accepted anything those shiny princesses did. Thankfully, they were good role models, but that's only sometimes the case with the characters our children are constantly bombarded with.

What goes into our children's hearts and minds through their eyes and ears impacts how they think, feel, grow, and act. It does influence their behavior, both in the immediate future and the long-term future.

According to a report by Common Sense Media, *The Media and Violence Report,*[19] "Boys who viewed TV violence heavily at age 6 were more likely to manifest violent behavior at age 19.

The researchers visited the same participants years later when they were 30 years old and found a correlation between early exposure to TV violence and self-reports of adult aggression, including criminal behavior."

I've used two examples of aggression and violence, but this also applies to the language used. I have two little girls, so "sassy talk", and the way characters speak to each other and adults in the show is one behavior that I am specifically attuned to. From a young age, I've had to explain to my girls why they aren't allowed to watch certain popular TV shows, generally ones based on toy characters.

I explained to them that the way that the ponies or puppies talk to each other in that show is not being a good friend. "They use mean and sassy words to talk to their friends, and I don't want you to learn to talk like that to your friends. That's why you can't watch that show."

It is only sometimes the case, but often, shows and movies that come from toys are less high-quality and shows and movies that come from literature or true stories tend to be more high-quality.

The key influence that TV and movie characters have (as well as kids on YouTube that our children watch) is why it is so vital that the shows we allow them "into" are high-quality "friendships" for them to spend time with. This can be a huge benefit to us, as we spoon-feed our children high-quality content, but it can also mean that lower-quality content can be detrimental.

When our children are young and living in our home, we get to choose what goes into their eyes and, thus, into their hearts and minds. We get to choose the "grid" they see the world through, and we get to decide if that grid is straight or crooked. This grid is influenced by their "TV friends", YouTubers they watch, video game narratives, and anyone they interact with online.

To small children, when they are watching *Daniel Tiger*, *Wild Kratz*, or *Bluey*, those characters are their friends, their peers, and what they say must be true. Older children and teens feel the same way about what and who they see on their screens. Children don't have the filter we have of "Oh, that's a cartoon. Of course, this is not real." They absorb the content, not necessarily the context.

One of my favorite children's books is *The Paper Dolls* by Julia Donaldson. In this book, a little girl and her mother make some paper dolls, and the dolls go on various adventures throughout the little girl's day. At one point, she loses them, and the book says that they flew... "into the little girl's memory where they found white mice and fireworks, and a starfish soap, and a kind granny, and the butterfly hairslide, and more and more lovely things each day and each year."

The beautiful illustration on this page shows a magical forest with all those things inside of it and more. It's such a lovely view of what we can fill a child's memory with, things true, beautiful, excellent, lovely. I always cry when I get to this point, partly because I've lost my kind granny and partly because it stirs me with a passion to fill my daughters' memories with beautiful things. Their hearts and minds are treasure boxes, the part of them that we get to store up with treasures.

One of the joys of parenting is that we get to reshape the world for our children. We get to decide what they learn first, what they focus on, and how they interpret the world. One of the ways we do this is by choosing the kind of TV, games, and other media that goes into their minds when they are young. They are sponges absorbing it all.

Let's choose the best, the most beautiful, the truest, the most interesting, and the most amazing things to show them instead of the cheap fast laughs, saucy, flirty teens, and poorly drawn cartoons.

I like to think of media intake as food. The things that are best for them, the richest in nutrients, I give them a lot of. High-quality books, nature documentaries (when I can get the girls to watch them), or educational television, they can have more of.

Fast laughs and flashy pictures with no content are like sugar, they can have a little bit of this, but it won't be the main part of their diet.

How do we decide what our children can intake in our homes? What grid are we looking through when a new show pops up on the TV, or their friends are all playing a new game or adding a new app?

Here's something that's helped me. I like to ask two questions when evaluating media for my family.

1. What does it treasure? Does this media/ show/ game/ app treasure the same things we treasure as a family?

2. What does it scorn? Does this media scorn the good, true, and beautiful? Or does it scorn values that are important to our family?

Ultimately, are our highly-held beliefs disrespected in this show or game, or are they upheld?

An easy way to assess the show's substance is to watch it with your eyes closed and listen to the dialogue, the intensity level of the music, and what kinds of words are used. It becomes a lot easier to see the truth of what a show is teaching when we aren't distracted by the beautiful, flashing lights and characters.

We become what we behold, so let's put the best, the most beautiful, and the truest things before our children's eyes while we are the ones holding the remote. Train their tastes to crave good food.

Chapter Ten Grace Note:

I've often found myself down a rabbit hole of "less than the best" TV for my girls, usually during sickness or bad weather when we have more screen time. The great news is it's always possible to change the channel. My girls recently got into watching old-school cartoons, which seemed harmless but ended up with them laughing every time a character got hurt.

After a few weeks of them watching it, I decided that maybe this wasn't the best for them, so I told them. I explained that since really what they were watching wasn't the best (laughing at someone getting hurt), we were going to take a break. They fussed a little bit but moved on.

We don't always know how a certain media or technology will impact our kids, but if we hear sassy attitudes or extra fighting after a while, or if they seem more angsty or irritable, we can take the screens away and see if that helps. It's a learning process, just like with food, and there is so much grace.

So don't stress if every show is the most perfect show ever; observe how things impact your children and make small changes as you see fit. Any growth is just that – growth.

"I did not wish to live what was not life;
living is so dear."

-Henry David Thoreau

Walden
1854

Chapter Eleven

Boredom and Walt Disney

A young father sat on a park bench. He squinted across the pavement at his two young daughters riding an amusement park ride supervised by their mother. The entire atmosphere of the amusement park was seedy, greasy, and unkempt. Food wrappers blew across the ground, and the rides needed a new coat of paint. The man ate his peanuts from a paper bag and thought to himself, surely we can do better. What if there was a better place to bring your children on a Sunday afternoon?

Within 15 minutes, a new image filled his mind, a beautiful park, clean, well-kept, safe and friendly, welcoming and warm. "What if a place like that existed?" he thought. Then, his family approached. Walt Disney smiled, stood up, and joined his family to walk to the next ride. Many years later, Disneyland opened, and its doors have been open ever since, welcoming families from around the world into just such a place. A place that he first conceived in a moment of waiting, a moment of boredom, even perhaps, many years before.

When I first read that story[20] in a biography about his life, I thought to myself, "I'm so glad Walt Disney didn't have a smartphone." If Walt had a smartphone in his pocket on that fateful day, he might have hit the high score on candy crush, but the dream of Disneyland may never have happened. And it may have; we don't know. But that's just the point. We don't know. We don't know what amazing ideas could happen when we get bored if we don't let ourselves get bored.

Since I've become a mom, I've always had a smartphone; for any mother who has had children in the last 20 years, this is likely true of them as well. Moms have smartphones now.

Jess Johnston, who writes a blog called *Wonderoak*, has this to say about what Moms need: Friends. Moms need friends. That's what we need.

But how do we make friends? In the olden days, Moms would go to Mom things like the library and the park and church Bible studies. At those places, they would meet other moms, and one mom would say, "Want to come over to my house?" the other mom would say, "Yes, please," and they would become friends.

I don't know about you, but when I go to the park, 90% of the time, every adult is looking at their phone or child. The "I'll just look around the playground and make small talk with strangers" thing is not very cool. This makes it hard to initiate a conversation and make friends. So, our constant distraction from ourselves leaves no opening for us to connect with the people right in front of us, which lends more and more to our feelings of isolation.

This past year, I did a book study on my blog and social media, studying the book *Bored and Brilliant* by Manoush Zomorodi[21], and it was excellent. Manoush's thesis is that when we are "bored", our brains come up with our most "brilliant" ideas, but we often fill up those "boring" times with scrolling on our phones (or even movies and tv), and we miss our flashes of brilliance.

In the book, she has a challenge for each chapter, which is meant to be done all in one week after the book's completion. This is the "Bored and Brilliant Challenge." I did this challenge week on my blog, and it was fantastic. I created a similar challenge, changing a few days to fit what we'd discussed during the book study. Here were the weekly challenges:

MONDAY

Keep your phone in your bag or a drawer,
not your pocket or on your person.

TUESDAY

No Photo Day (or take 1 photo of the day).

WEDNESDAY

Delete "that" app you use the most or
put your phone screen on black and white for the day.

THURSDAY

Stay off social media and the news until noon.

FRIDAY

Spend 5 minutes watching your world (without a phone in
hand) and then record what you see and notice.

SATURDAY

Think of a problem. Spend 30 minutes "getting bored,"
then return to the problem with a pencil and paper.

SUNDAY

Rest and Reflect.

It's a great challenge and I highly recommend it. I also recommend you read *Bored and Brilliant*. Doing this challenge helped me see how much the "cracks" in my day can get easily filled in with distraction when I need to think and process my life.

Zomorodi explains this, saying, "When we let ourselves space out, and our minds wander, we do our most original thinking and problem solving; without distraction, your mind can go to some interesting and unexpected places. Creativity needs a push, and boredom, which allows new and different connections to form in our brain, is a most effective muse."

Allowing myself time to think, to look out the window for a few minutes rather than read the latest news article, has been a huge benefit for me.

When something is bothering me, playing on the fringes of my mind uncomfortably, my knee-jerk response can often be to distract myself, watch a quick YouTube clip, or get lost in a Netflix show, but what I'm learning is that that niggling feeling is my brain saying "I need time to think about and process this thing." If I give myself the time to think and process and lean into it, my thoughts often beautifully detangle themselves, especially if I invite God into the process and let Him help me think it out.

The most common example of this is when it's time for me to do the dishes. There have been seasons when I could only make myself do the dishes if I had the iPad in front of me and an episode of a funny TV show on. But other times, when I use that time to let myself think through whatever I need to think through, it can be super helpful and even fun to think through ideas and problems and issues that have been rumbling around my head all day.

I'm so enjoying the feeling of getting my head back, getting my thoughts back, and having my ideas and the inner world be a wonderful place to be, and this all happened because I started allowing "free space" and "boredom" back into my life.

One strategy to re-train our brains to be comfortable with "boredom" is the 3-minute breathing break.

Find a spot near where you tend to get stressed. Maybe it's your car; maybe it's your pantry; maybe it's outside.

Try to be hidden so no one finds you (they will eventually, but try.)

Take a deep breath and let it out.

Then do it again several times.

Slow breathing sends a message to your brain to calm down. There are nerves on your lungs that send messages to your brain, so when they sense your slow breathing, they send a message to your racing brain that you aren't in distress; you don't need to run away from a jaguar. You are fine. Doing this for a few minutes can biologically calm down your brain.

"Life is never made unbearable by circumstances, but only by lack of meaning and purpose."

– Viktor Frankl

Man's Search for Meaning
1946

Chapter Twelve

Finding Meaning in our Lives

How to Never Paint an Apple: (Based on a True Story)

Step 1: Decide to paint an apple
Step 2: Get on Pinterest
Step 3: Become overwhelmed with everyone else's perfect apples
Step 4: Try a tutorial one time and fail horribly
Step 5: Give up and never paint an apple

Sometimes the online world meant to instruct and inspire instead overwhelms and discourages. This can be true in far more important matters than apple painting, such as marriage, parenting, creating a home, and choosing a life path.

It's interesting how quickly we can go from "I'd like to learn about this" to "I'll never do it as well as them; I'll not even try." The internet contains high-quality photos, videos, reels, and TikTok. It's full of things that seem like they don't take very long to make, but they do.

Imagine my surprise the first time I tried to make an Instagram reel. Surely, 30 seconds of content couldn't take too long to complete. But there was so much involved, setting up my camera, finding the right light, filming each section (more than once), finding music, adding words, editing, captioning, and posting.

It was 2 hours before I had finished it. This wasn't very encouraging because, although I felt like it was a decent reel, it seemed to take longer than it should.

I know that others also spend a long time on their "Insta" lives. It's a fact of life that nothing done well happened "Insta"-ntly.

Let's press on this issue. We have discussed apples and Instagram reels (TikToks, Facebook Reels or YouTube "shorts"). What about actual living? What does this concept have to say to our real lives?

I won't be the only mother of young children to have spent a difficult evening of bedtime tears and protests, only to hop online to view the perfectly styled or perfectly imperfect photos and videos and captions of a friend or influencer. It's discouraging to see that while I suffer, they seem only to thrive. We KNOW it's not the truth, but we FEEL it might be. They might be better at life than we are.

It's in the weak moments that we often need a break, and we jump to social media, the internet, or even TV to find our rest, only to discover that we are failing at that which matters most to us - our home and motherhood, our families that we are sacrificing and giving for. We are failing them! At least, it seems like it when we are surrounded by a mix of dirty, plastic, colorful dishes in the sink at 9pm while Mama Instagram prances in a dried grass field with her brood of five children all dressed in tan ("link in bio for outfit details").

This is very important.

Listen to what I am about to say.

The more we pour our mind and energy into social media, the poorer our mental health will become because our mental health is inextricably linked to our meaning in life. Read that again.

The more we pour our mind and energy into social media, the poorer our mental health will become because our mental health is inextricably linked to our meaning in life.

Often, social media convinces us that what we are doing, our small acts of love, sacrifice, home care, and childcare, are not valid ways to spend our lives. Our work is too small, our parenting is done too imperfectly, and our lives (compared to this big, bold world of shiny happy people) hold no meaning or not enough importance to matter. We want to count, and that's ok. We should want to matter.

One afternoon recently, I went to a birthday party at a local playground. The long winter's drizzle and rain had made the past few weeks miserable and wet, but that day, for the first time, the bright sunshine broke through, warming the air and cheering our hearts with the promise of spring soon to come. Tiny green buds were pressing through the worn brown bark on the trees, and birds sang merrily in the sky above.

Little girls in party dresses and boys in soccer clothes ran to and fro while at least ten lovely young moms in spring dresses, pastels, and linen white stood around and chatted about the glorious weather and generally caught up on each other's lives. I stood in my pink floral dress and chunky pink cardigan and chatted with the best of them, revelling in the joy of the presence of friends and the beautiful moment we were sharing. It was lovely.

Then, that night I sat on the couch scrolling on my phone and stumbled onto an article called "*My Body Style*" about various color palettes and what clothes I should wear for the body and face that I've been given.

Ten minutes spread into an hour as I researched capsule wardrobes, "warm spring", and various things that might look as good on me as Jennifer Anniston. As I searched, an interesting phenomenon occurred in my mind. My thoughts wandered back to the lovely afternoon at the park, and I suddenly wondered what "style" my friends had. I wondered how they had so easily, it seemed, figured out how to wear clothes that were just right for them, and I suddenly saw myself as an overgrown 13-year-old in contrast.

They had picked out just the right clothes; *They* certainly knew their exact style and had probably known it for years, which is why *their* lives had turned out so well. On the other hand, I was nearly 40 and still figuring it all out. So, I continued to scroll and spiral until I had enough.

Slightly dizzied, I picked up a book that my sister had recommended, a book that was the best seller in the wake of World War 2. It was *Man's Search for Meaning* by Viktor Frankl[22], an Austrian doctor who had, along with his family, survived the concentration camps. He wrote his masterpiece about his experiences there and his observations on the importance of having a purpose and meaning in life. Seeing life as being valuable gives people the ability to push through dark and trying times, even as dark as a concentration camp.

The chapter I was reading was entitled *Experiences in a*

Concentration Camp. Anyone who has read WW2 history concerning the camps will inevitably be familiar with the sufferings. The eminent threat of death, the cold, snowy marches in bare or nearly bare feet. The starvation, the beatings, the insults, the gas chambers. My "body type" suddenly didn't seem to matter so much.

He wrote how nine men shared one bed, each bed a bare wooden platform, one after another stacked high in the room. They had two blankets to share and no pillows, although some men snuck their (wet, muddy) shoes into their beds to use as a pillow.

Inconceivable suffering.

Just as I read this, my daughter got out of bed. She wanted the lullaby music in her room turned up louder.

My mind turned from the cold winter of 1945 in Auschwitz to my daughter's cozy warm bedroom. She had two blankets all to herself and two pillows; her soft bed, a loving mother to comfort her, the rosy round cheeks of a child well fed, well loved. I told her these things. I gently shared with her the story of the men who had slept nine to a bed, only two blankets to share and shoes for pillows. I told her how cozy and warm her room was and how loved she was. She snuggled down and fell asleep.

Then, I began to ponder this thing, the events of the day — the picture-perfect party in the park, the lovely moms, my comparison of myself to these women — and then, the stark reality of human suffering, and I realized why we must read deeply and well, both of great sorrow and great delight. Reading of great delight allows us to expand our minds and souls to soak in the true beauty of life around us. Reading poems about dewdrops and rainbows and love and joy, reading great and noble stories, giving our imagination the ability to fly away from where we find ourselves and point out to us the beauty of the moment we are in – this is valuable work. But the reading of suffering, done well, carries great weight and purpose for our souls and minds. It allows us to see the vast variety of human life, that while there is great delight and joy, there also truly can be great, deep suffering. There IS great, deep suffering beyond what the average person ever dips their toe into.

The moms I chatted with at the park that day have far more in common with me than differences. They, too, tucked their children in that night with more blankets than necessary, plenty of pillows, and every child on their own mattress. They, too, have enough food in their fridge and are safe at night, home with their families.

Let me tell you why this was such a big revelation for me.
I could spend the next 20 years of my life running in circles, trying to compete with other women who, in all reality, are just like me. We've all done it in certain seasons of our lives, spotting a friend who seemed to have it all and trying to mold our lives to look like hers, while in most reality, it already basically did.

We tend to spend time around people like us, but sometimes we twist and turn until we find ourselves focusing on what is different instead. And this distracts us. It distracts us from the great joy of that other person. It distracts us from the great joy of our own lives, and more soberingly, it distracts us from the needs of others around us who might need our attention, others who might truly BE in great suffering. Playing dress up and trying to win at the "Mommy Game" pales in comparison.

That night, I was challenged by my shallow evening activity (not wrong but not deep or constructive) and the contrast with the true, deep reading I did next. I realized that a lifetime of shallow reading sets me up for a shallow life, a shallow life of comparison and never measuring up — A lifetime of being thinly distracted by trivial matters while the real world marches by.

What if we all, women with homes and children and enough blankets, spend our days and extra energies trying to compete with one another while a world in need cries out for real help?
The distracted suburban moms of our time faces alight with screens, distracted by blips and 30-minute trends, exhausting ourselves to the point where meaningful work and relationships seem like "too much." While reading deeply and well brings into stark relief the layers of safety and blessing I sat upon that night.

There's nothing wrong with finding out your body type, taking BuzzFeed quizzes, or scrolling social media daily. And sure, maybe there's not. But it's worth considering if these activities lead us to a deeper, richer life or not. And if not, what could?

This is also a balance. When I am tired and giving out a lot in my daily life and work, I need something lighter, something funny, something easy to ingest to help me get my mind off my struggles. But it's also worth stepping back occasionally and checking our trajectory to ensure our fun and easy activities aren't leading to a shallowing of mind and shortening of attention span over time. And if we find they are, we can make adjustments. This is what all of life is, adjustments.

We don't have to feel guilty about every moment we spend scrolling social media instead of reading *The Illiad*. But if we feel purposeless and even hopeless, it's worth considering taking a break from shallow distractions like this and seeing if that helps us regain our sense of self and purpose in the world.

When we believe our lives have meaning, we as humans can suffer bravely and live through the very worst things in life. But it's when we lose that sense of purpose in our lives we suffer most, give up, and decide, "What is the actual point?" And depression and mental health issues come to sit on us.

I think this is fabulous to know because a) I also believe God has a plan for us. This isn't a "Western construct" or happy theology, it's Biblically true, and b) this is something we can walk towards. We can walk towards the meaning we will find rather than scroll ourselves into distraction, believing others have the meaning we must copy or submit to.

So, let's end this book with this, our lives do have meaning. God has a plan for our lives, and we are made for a life of purpose. When we now hear the whisper of "Why try? You'll never reach their level of apple painting or reel making or family photo taking," it might be a good time to take a break from that kind of on-screen input and spend some time considering your own life and values.

Spend time alone, sorting out your thoughts and some of the meaningful things in your life. I've provided some pages at the end of this book to help this process along for you. First you'll find a mind map to visually see the valuable things in your life. Write your name in the center of a piece of paper and circle it. Then, write the names of the important people in your life, values, hobbies, vocation and work. Circle these, then draw lines that connect the things that connect. Feel free to draw your own if you prefer.

Next, go to the Priority Circles page. Put your most important relationships in the center, then the next most important value in the next round and so on. This is a great way to see your priorities this season; what do you want to invest your time into?

Finally ask yourself, what do I want to invest my time into? Use the third page to visually organize your values and priorities into a list. It's possible to spend our highest amount of energy on the least important values. Take some time to examine what your highest values truly are. Consider posting them somewhere in your home where you'll see them often, to remember the things that are the most important to you.

Together, let us learn over time to live with those things as the focus of our days, allowing the happy shiny photos on the internet to be happy and shiny but not giving them the power to throw us off our values and precious course.

Epilogue

It's 4:40 pm on a Friday afternoon in June. Down here in the Southern Hemisphere, it's early winter, the golden sun is casting its last rays across the sea, and the still, cool air is fresh and crisp. We've come to the end of the week, the end of the day, the end of this book.

Looking back over the last five years of learning about the digital age and parenting, I realize a few final things. 1. I'm often too hard on myself. 2. Parenting my children is more about what I DO with them than rules of what NOT to do. 3. Relationships are what we want, and they aren't that complicated after all.

Yes, we live in the "Digital Age", just as Jane Austen lived in the "Georgian Era", but that doesn't encompass all of who we are and how we live.

The last five years have seen a global pandemic and a shift of online culture from "hustle" and "be a girl boss" to homesteading and baking bread; people are getting chickens, returning to the soil, to a slow way of living.

Life's a pendulum, after all, and often what one generation too highly prizes, the next generation will reject.

So I'm not afraid for our children and their children. I'm not scared that robots will take the sky and rain down hellfire. I'm not. Our generation will sow seeds of slow living, peaceful friendship, and intentional creativity into our children, and we will reap a harvest of good fruit from that in our lifetime and beyond.

We get to decide what kind of life we live, what environment we create in our homes, and what kind of relationships we cultivate, and we are empowered to do this in whatever world we find ourselves in today.

We are raising the children of the digital age, but we are also raising children who love the earth, swim in the sea, love the smell of the forest, climb, laugh, and play. And the important thing is, that WE are raising them. We are the educators, we pave the way for them to understand the world, we walk with them, talk with them, teach them worldview, share what we love with them and teach them wisdom along the way.

I once sat in the car near a windy beach with my sick child; she was too unwell to go on a walk with her Daddy and sister, so she and I sat together in the parking lot while they walked. Directly in front of me was a little tree, blowing in the strong sea breeze, branches bobbing this way and that. It leaned a bit in the wind, but it wasn't uprooted. Long days and nights, that sapling had dug its roots deep into the cliff of dirt, woven its tangled legs around rocks and sought water down in the earth so that now, no matter how strong the winds blew, it stood strong.

This picture stuck with me because this is what I want for my children in life; it's what I want for myself. I want deep roots, going down into the earth, living, seeking water to drink, absorbing nutrients from the good soil. Then, no matter how strong the winds blow, we will stand fast.

So let's go forth in love, not fear, harvesting the best of the world and sowing it into our homes for our families and filling their memories with treasures. Yes, we will watch tv and use technology, but we will also ramble in the woods, go for walks around our neighborhoods, and spend time with friends. It's not either-or; it's both, and it all adds up to a glorious life in a wonderful world.

Thanks for coming along friends,

Heather

To find more resources and encouragement, check out www.digimummy.com

References

Chapter 2: Influencer Culture and Me

1. Kat Tenbarge. *Young influencers are being offered cheap procedures in return for promotion. They say it's coming at a cost.* NBC News, April 29, 2022. Retrieved from https://www.nbcnews.com/tech/internet/followers-cheaper-lips-young-influencers-detail-allure-cosmetic-proced-rcna14463

Chapter 3: Trying to Be Everywhere at Once

2. Neri Oxman, *Abstract: The Art of Design*, Netflix, 2019

3. Rob Barry, Georgia Wells, John West, Joanna Stern, and Jason French. *How TikTok Serves Up Sex and Drug Videos to Minors.* Wall Street Journal, Sept 8, 2021. Retrieved from https://www.wsj.com/articles/tiktok-algorithm-sex-drugs-minors-11631052944

Chapter 4: Service vs. Celebrity

4. The Harris Poll, 2019. Retrieved from https://theharrispoll.com/briefs/lego-group-kicks-off-global-program-to-inspire-the-next-generation-of-space-explorers-as-nasa-celebrates-50-years-of-moon-landing/

5. Mikaela Wilkes. *Friend's actor Lisa Kudrow admits she Hated being a Celebrity.* Stuff.co.nz. October 25, 2020. Retrieved from https://i.stuff.co.nz/entertainment/celebrities/123203138/friends-actor-lisa-kudrow-admits-she-hated-being-a-celebrity

Chapter 5: What's an iPhone?

6. Cal Newport. *Digital Minimalism*. 2019.

7. Simon Sinek. *The Millennial Question*. December 31, 2016. Retrieved from https://www.youtube.com/watch?v=vudaAYx2IcE

Chapter 6: Why We're Addicted to Our Phones

8. Cal Newport. *Why You Should Quit Social Media.* TED. September 20, 2016. Retrieved from https://www.ted.com/talks/cal_newport_why_you_should_quit_social_media?language=en

9. Adam Altar. *Irresistable*. 2017. Page 17.

10. Manoush Zomorodi. *Bored and Brilliant*. 2017. "The default mode, a term coined by [Marcus]Raischle is used to describe the brain "at rest." p.35-39.

11. Manoush Zomorodi. *Bored and Brilliant*. 2017. "When we lose focus on the outside world and drift inward, we're not shutting down. We're tapping into a vast trove of memories, dissecting our interactions with other people, and reflecting on who we are." p.37.

Chapter 8: Stress Knitting

12. Malaka Gharib, *Feeling Artsy? Here's How Making Art Helps Your Brain*. 2020. Retrieved from https://www.npr.org/sections/health-shots/2020/01/11/795010044/feeling-artsy-heres-how-making-art-helps-your-brain

13. Girija Kaimal, Hasan Ayaz, Joanna Herres, Rebekka Dieterich-Hartwell, Bindal Makwana, Donna H. Kaiser and Jennifer A. Nasser. *Functional near-infrared spectroscopy assessment of reward perception based on visual self-expression: Coloring, doodling, and free drawing*. The Arts in Psychotherapy, Volume 55, 2017, Pages 85-92, ISSN 0197-4556. https://www.sciencedirect.com/science/article/pii/S019745561630171X

14. *The Crown*. Season 1, Episode 5. Netflix. 2016

Chapter 9: No Fear in Love

15. John 8:32. *The Holy Bible*.

Chapter 10: The Grid and the treasure box

16. Angela C. Santomero. *Preschool Clues*. 2018. p.188 -189.

17. https://www.simplypsychology.org/bobo-doll.html

18. Angela C. Santomero. *Preschool Clues.* 2018. p.196

19. Common Sense Media. *Media and Violence, an Analysis of Current Research.* Winter 2013. Retrieved from https://www.commonsensemedia.org/sites/default/files/research/report/media-and-violence-research-brief-2013.pdf. p.12.

Chapter 11: Boredom and Walt Disney

20. Bob Thomas. *Walt Disney: An American Original.* 1976.

21. Manoush Zamorodi. *Bored and Brilliant.* 2017.

Chapter 12: Finding Meaning in Our Lives

22. Viktor Frankl. *Man's Search for Meaning.* 2011.

About the Author

Heather Lake is a Midwest girl who found herself living by the sea. Raised by a Tech-Whiz Dad and a Gardener Mom, she is a digital native and a dirt-loving free spirit.

She loves reading classic children's literature and hiking in the freshest air she can find on the weekends with her Kiwi husband and two daughters.

Mind Map

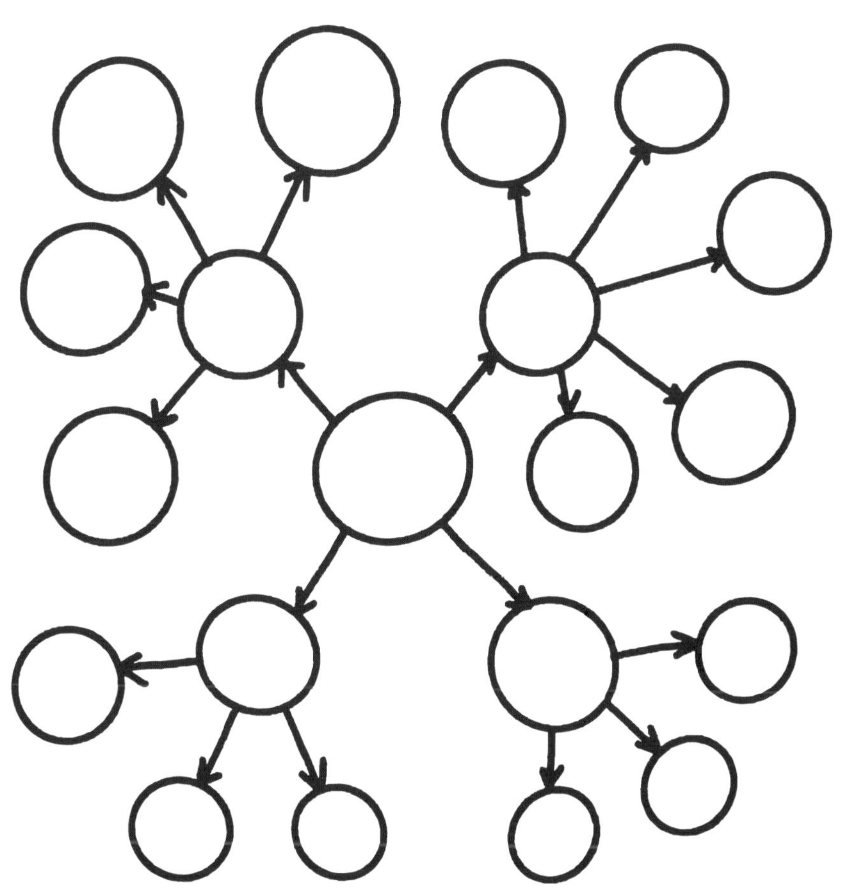

My Priorities

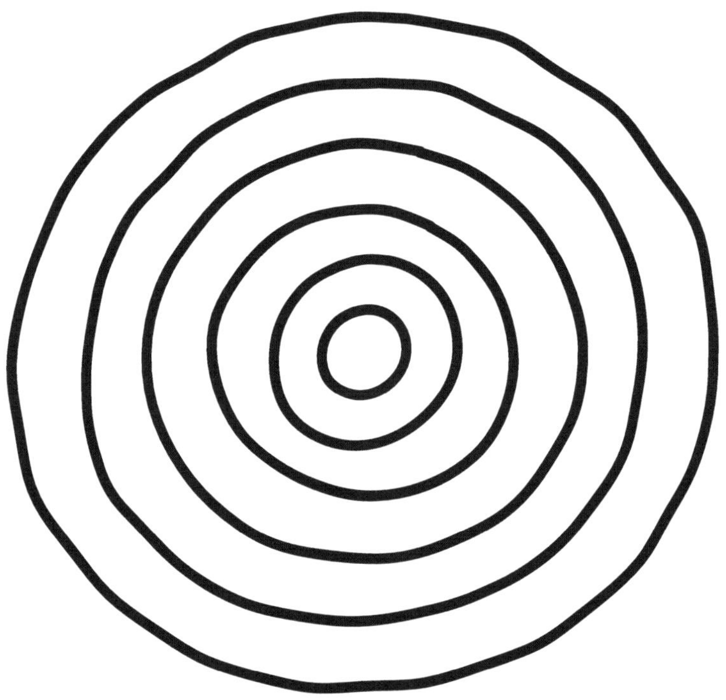

Use these circles to organize your priorities in this season. List the demands in your time and key relationships, then write them on the circles in order of priority, starting with the most important at the center and working your way out.

My Values

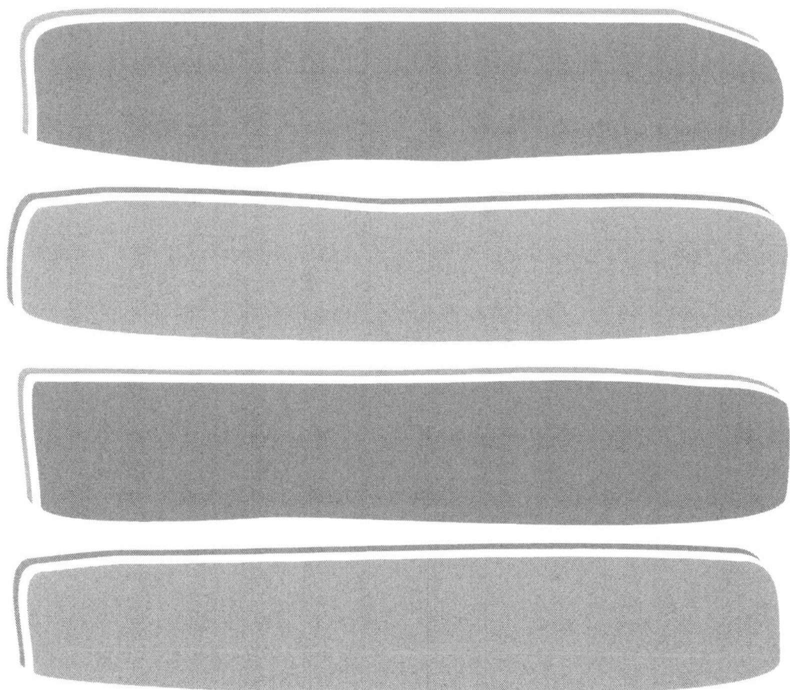

Made in the USA
Monee, IL
14 August 2023